SHORTCUTS TO SL

Maps and Photographs

Junior Certificate Geography

Fiona Fay

GILL & MACMILLAN

Gill & Macmillan Ltd
Hume Avenue
Park West
Dublin 12
with associated companies throughout the world
www.gillmacmillan.ie

© Fiona Fay 2005
0 7171 3739 2

Colour reproduction by Typeform Repro
Print origination in Ireland by Design Image
Illustrations by Design Image

The paper used in this book is made from the wood pulp of managed forests.
For every tree felled, at least one tree is planted, thereby renewing natural resources.

Acknowledgments
For permission to reproduce photographs and other copyrighted material the author
and publisher gratefully acknowledge the following:
73B, 89B © Aerofilms; 72, 76R, 78, 81B, 82, 84, 86, 88, 94, 95R, 95L, 96T, 96B, 98,
99, 100, 109, 115, 118, 121 © Peter Barrow; 1 © Corbis; 43 © Kevin Dwyer;
Lonely Planet Images: 31B © Richard Mills; 35 © Eoin Clarke; 36B © Gareth
McCormack; 31T, 36T © John Cleare/Mountain Camera Picture Library; 73T, 77B, 80,
81T, 85, 90 © Finbar O'Connell; 76L, 77T, 77C, 79, 112 © Ordnance Survey Ireland.
Ordnance Survey Maps 'Based on Survey Ireland Permit No. 7903' © Ordnance
Survey Ireland and Government of Ireland.
The author and publisher have made every effort to trace all copyright holders, but if
any has been inadvertently overlooked we would be pleased to make the necessary
arrangements at the first opportunity.

Contents

Chapter **1**
An introduction to maps

Mapping of Ireland

Ireland was of great interest to map makers in ancient times as it was the most westerly point in Europe. In the second century AD Ptolemy, the great map maker, was able to get enough information about Ireland to list the lines of latitude and longitude of sixty features in Ireland including mountains and lakes.

Ireland began to be mapped in more detail with the Plantations. Cartographers (map makers) followed armies into the areas taken. They drew up regional maps to help with dividing out the land among the English Planters.

The first world maps were inaccurate as they were drawn up from information given by sailors who were afraid of sailing too far from the coast as they thought they might fall off the edge of the earth.

Map of Ireland from 1596

This is a drawing of the world map given to the explorer Christopher Columbus. He set off in 1492 to prove that the world was round.

What was wrong or missing from the map?

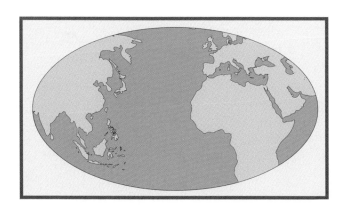

One of the oldest maps in the world was drawn on a tablet of clay over 4,000 years ago by a tax collector. He needed to know how much land people owned so that he could collect tax from them. Instead of writing a list he drew a map.

The era of European exploration gave map makers a wealth of new information which allowed them to make more accurate and detailed maps.

Maps are very accurate nowadays. Aerial photographs, ones which are taken from an aeroplane, can give us a clear picture of an area of country. Satellite pictures show even larger areas. These are used to make up-to-date modern maps. The Ordnance Survey Office in Dublin produces detailed maps of every part of Ireland.

Scale

A plan is a bird's eye view of an object or building that is viewed from directly above. It shows you where things are placed. A bird's eye has the full view of things. To draw a bird's eye view of Ireland you would need a very large page, hundreds of kilometres long and wide. So the drawing is reduced or drawn to *scale*.

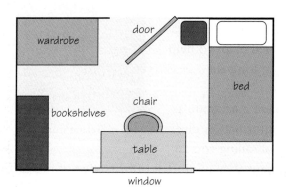

Plan of a bedroom
(not drawn to scale)

Try drawing a plan or bird's eye view of your own bedroom or your classroom.

Scale means that a certain distance on the map stands for a certain distance in reality.

For example: In a 1:50,000 map, for every one part on the map there are 50,000 parts in reality; or to put it another way, for every 1 cm on the map there are 2 km in reality on the ground. (We will look at scale in more detail in Chapter 2.)

There are maps of every different shape, size and *scale*.

World　　　　　　　Europe　　　　　　　Ireland

Why study maps?

Maps are important to many people in the work that they do. The builder, weather forecaster, sailor and pilot are some people who use maps. Can you think of any more?

We use maps in many ways:
* to find our way when lost
* to plan our holidays
* in our spare time on a walk or hike
* when orienteering and on treasure hunts.

Keywords are words you need to know and understand.

Keywords			
Directions	Scale	Linear scale	Symbol
Grid reference	Relief	Drainage	

Directions

North, south, east and west are the main directions.
These directions help us to give the location of features on a map.

Scale
Scale shows the distance on a map that stands for a greater distance in reality.

Linear scale
A way of showing scale: a line divided into kilometres or miles.

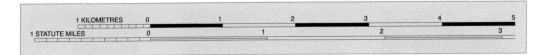

Symbol
  A small picture that stands for something on the map. Symbols are used instead of words.

Grid references
A way of giving exact locations of features. A grid reference is made up of letters and numbers.

O 139 862

L 42 29

Relief
The shape and height of the earth's surface.

Drainage
The way in which water is taken from the land's surface naturally.

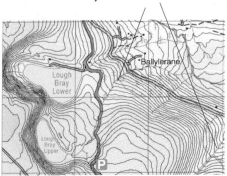

Keywords

Across

2. A scale line divided into kilometres or miles
7. The way in which water is taken from the land's surface naturally
9. These help us to give a general location of features

Down

1. This picture replaces words
3. A way of giving exact locations of features; Grid _____
4. A certain distance on the map stands for a greater distance in reality
5. The shape and height of the earth's surface
6. A main direction N
8. A main direction W

Now find the answers in the word search, and also find the other two main directions which were not in the crossword.

E	T	S	E	W	R	L	R	D	D
S	G	U	T	A	C	S	M	I	X
P	R	A	E	S	O	E	R	L	E
J	E	N	N	U	A	E	S	O	N
O	I	S	T	I	C	E	I	B	O
L	B	H	C	T	A	Z	K	M	R
C	X	C	I	A	C	R	E	Y	T
N	W	O	Z	A	L	X	D	S	H
K	N	R	E	L	I	E	F	S	D
S	E	C	N	E	R	E	F	E	R

5

On a map, to the side, there is usually a North arrow which makes it easier to tell direction. North, south, east and west are the main compass points. Their order can be remembered by a rhyme using the first letters:

Never

Eat

Shredded

Wheat

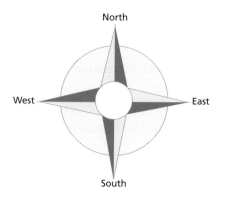

What part of Ireland do you live in?

Is that in the north, south, east or west of the country?

Look at the map of Ireland in an atlas. Fill in the blanks with the correct direction.

Galway is in the _____ of the country

Donegal is in the _____ of the country

Cork is in the _____ of the country

Kildare is in the _____ of the country

If you don't have a compass you can try to figure out directions during the day. The sun rises in the east, is directly south at midday and sets in the west.

You can also find directions on a clear night. Two of the stars which make up the group of stars known as the Plough are called pointers, above which is the bright North Star. When facing this you are facing north.

We can be more detailed in giving directions.

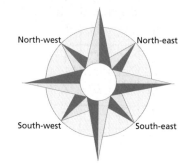

Follow the instructions below to finish a drawing on the grid. Begin at the star. The first in both A and B are done.

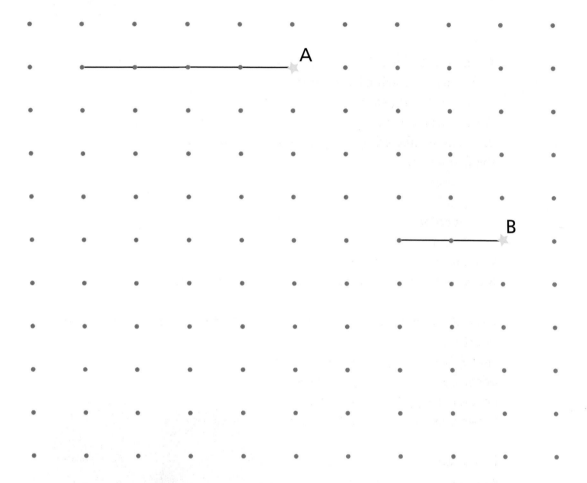

A. Draw a line starting at A going

1. 4 spaces west
2. 2 spaces south
3. 2 spaces east
4. 6 spaces south
5. 1 space south
6. 2 spaces east
7. 7 spaces north
8. 2 spaces east
9. 2 spaces north
10. 2 spaces west

B. Draw a line starting at B going

1. 2 spaces west
2. 1 space south
3. 1 space east
4. 1 space south-west
5. 1 space south
6. 2 spaces east
7. 1 space north
8. 1 space west
9. 1 space north-east
10. 1 space north.

Look at the map and symbols and answer the questions:

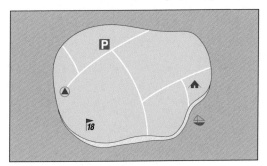

🅿 Parking	⛺ Camping
🏌 Golf course	⛵ Boating activities
🅨 Youth hostel	

1. What activity is off the south-east coast? _____

2. What activity is on the south-west of the island? _____

3. What **accommodation** is to the east of the island? _____

4. What does the symbol in the north of the island mean? _____

Accommodation means places to stay such as hostels and campsites (hotels and bed-and-breakfasts (B&Bs) are not marked on Ordnance Survey maps).

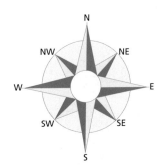

H	G	E
P	Y	O
A	R	G*

G   is north of R

E   is north-east of A

O   is _____ of P

G* is _____ of H

R   is _____ of A

A   is _____ of Y

P   is _____ of O

H   is _____ of R

Y   is _____ of E

Study the Ordnance Survey (OS) map and answer the questions that follow:

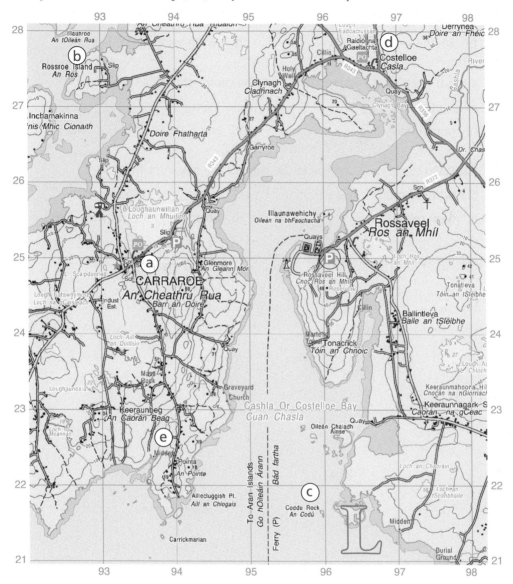

Find the parking symbol to the south-west of Rossaveel.

In what direction from this parking symbol is:

a) Carraroe _____

b) Rossroe Island _____

c) Coddu Rock _____

d) Raidió na Gaeltachta _____

e) Midden _____

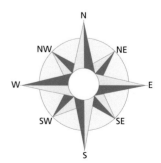

9

In what direction does the R343 road travel from Costelloe to Carraroe?

a) North-east ☐

b) South-west ☐

c) South ☐

d) North-west ☐

In what direction is Rossroe Island from the centre of Loch an Mhuilinn?

a) South-east ☐

b) North-west ☐

c) West ☐

d) North-east ☐

The R336 road from Costelloe to the edge of the map runs from

a) North to south ☐

b) West to east ☐

c) North-west to south-east ☐

d) North-east to south-west ☐

The direction from Rossaveel to the Mass Rock is _____

Chapter **3**
Scale and measuring distance

The scale on maps is shown in three different ways:

1. Representative fraction
2. Statement of scale
3. Linear scale.

Remember that all maps are drawn to scale. That means a certain distance on the map stands for a greater distance in reality.

Representative fraction 1:50,000 (RF) tells us that for every 1 unit of measurement on the map there are really 50,000.

Statement of scale says what the scale is. Here it is 2 cm to 1 km.

The distance from the post office in Headford south to Balrickard is 2 cm when you measure it on the map. So using the scale 2 cm : 1 km, it is a 1 km walk from the post office to Balrickard. What townland is a 1 km walk from the post office in a north-east direction?

Linear scale is a line divided into kilometres and parts of kilometres or miles.

Measurement using the linear scale

- Take a piece of paper with a straight edge.
- Line it up so that it passes through the two points you want to measure the distance between.
- Mark these two points carefully (A and B) on your paper.
- Line the paper up with the linear scale, with A at O kilometres, and read what the distance is to B.

Also known as 'As the crow flies'

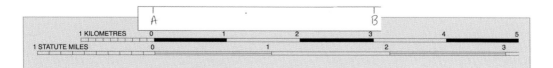

Measure the lengths of these lines using the linear scale. (Answer in km)

1. A_____B   1. = _____

2. A_____B   2. = _____

3. A_____B   3. = _____

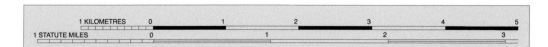

- Glenbeg
- Ballylin
- Castlemore
- Rathban
- Barrystown

Answer in km using the linear scale:

1. What is the distance from Glenbeg to Ballylin?

2. What is the distance from Rathban to Ballylin?

3. How far is it from Castlemore to Barrystown?

4. What is the length of the journey from Rathban to Castlemore, then on to Barrystown?

Measuring curved-line distances e.g. roads, railways, rivers

- Take a straight-edged piece of paper and mark your starting point A on both the paper and the map.
- Put the two together. At the first curve or 'turn' in the road mark where the road edge leaves the page. Mark this on your paper and map.
- Use this as your next turning point. Lining up the paper edge with the road, mark the next turn. Keep going until you reach your finish point. Mark as B.
- Use the linear scale to measure distance between A and B on the paper.

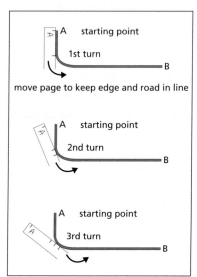

Measure the curved-line distance of the lines A and B. (Answers in km)

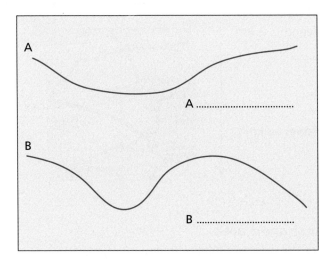

A ....

B ....

What is the length of the River Suir?

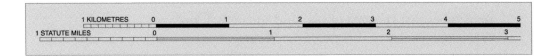

Calculating area

(Calculate = to work out)

To calculate regular areas

Ordnance Survey maps are divided into small boxes by thin blue lines; these boxes are called grid squares. Each grid square on a map with the scale 1:50,000 measures 2 cm on each side (its length and width). We know that 2 cm stands for 1 km in reality.

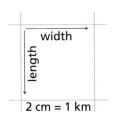

2 cm = 1 km

To get area you multiply length by width, so the area of a grid square is

1 km x 1 km = **1 km²**.

So to calculate the area of a regular shape:
Count the grid squares across (width): **2 km**
Count the grid squares down (length): **2 km**

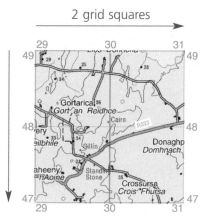

2 grid squares

Multiply your answers
$$2 \text{ km} \times 2 \text{ km} = \textbf{4 km}^2.$$

Don't forget to give your answer in km².

To calculate an irregular-shaped area

You may be asked to calculate the area of features that are irregularly shaped, such as a lake or a coastal area.

Remember that the area of one grid square is 1 km².

- Count all the grid squares that are at least half filled by the feature (tick them as you go along).
- Ignore the other squares.
- The number of squares that are at least half filled will give you the area of the feature.
  The area of the blue is 7 km²
  The area of the green is

  _____

Don't forget to give your answer in km².

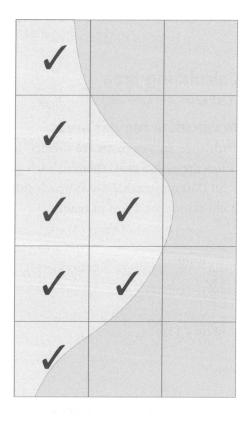

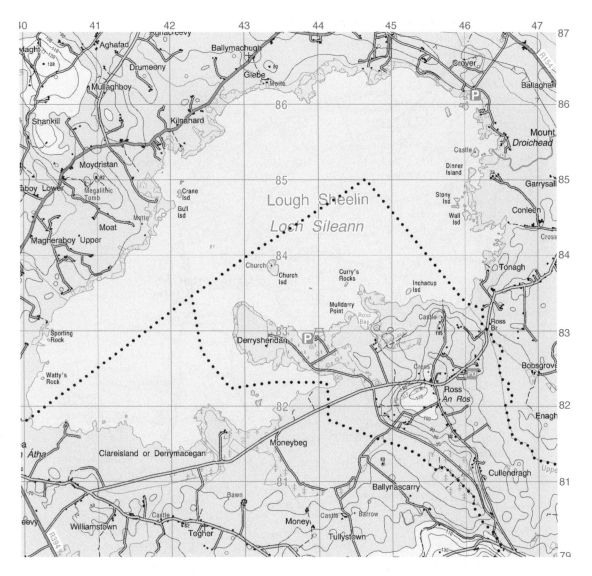

Calculate the area of Lough Sheelin: _____

Study the Ordnance Survey map of Skerries (page 16) and answer the following questions:

1. What is the length of this map in km?   _____

2. What is the width of this map in km?   _____

3. Calculate the area of this map extract.   _____

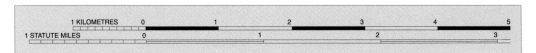

15

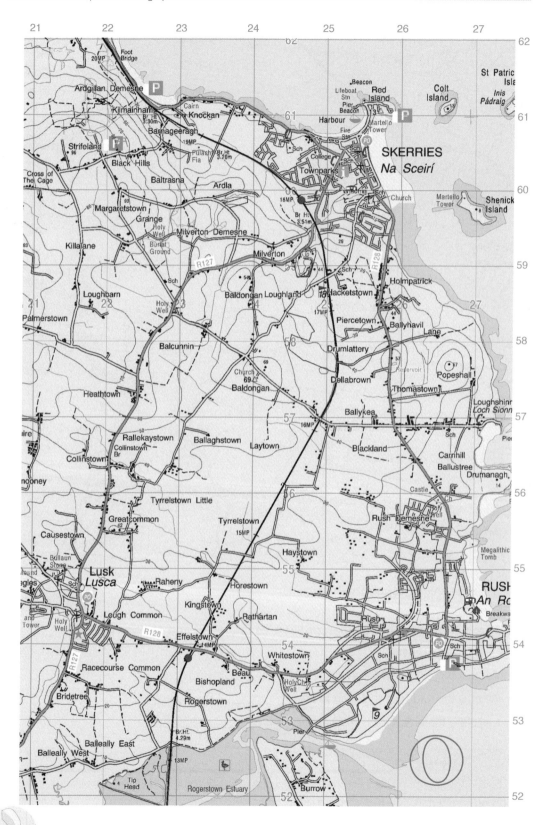

4. What is the distance in km from the post office in in Skerries to the post office in Lusk? _____

    PO = Post office

5. What is the distance in km from the post office in Skerries to the post office in Rush? _____

    Straight distance

6. Measure the distance in km along the R128 from the post office in Skerries to the post office in Rush. _____

7. Measure the distance in km along the railway line from the train station in Skerries to the one to the east of Lusk. _____

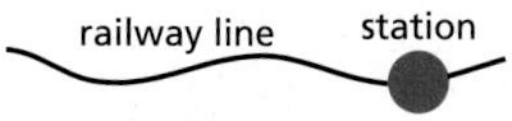

    railway line   station

    Curved-line measurement

8. Calculate the area in km² covered by the sea in the east of the map. _____

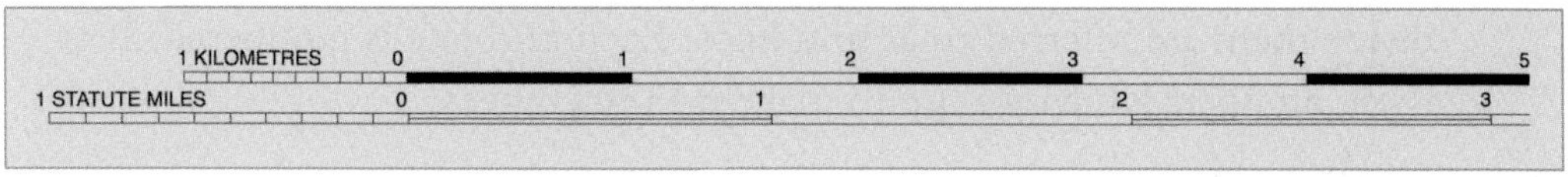

| 1 KILOMETRES | 0 | | 1 | | 2 | | 3 | | 4 | | 5 |
| 1 STATUTE MILES | 0 | | | 1 | | | 2 | | | 3 |

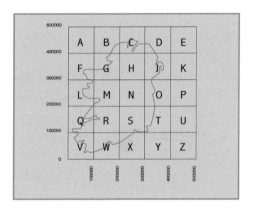

To help us locate or find things more easily on a map, the country of Ireland is divided up into a group of twenty-five squares, known as sub zones, which cover the country. Each has a letter and measures 100 km long and 100 km wide.

Look at the map of Ireland in an atlas. What counties are in the sub zones of the following letters?

O _____   M _____

R _____   W _____

Each sub zone is divided into 100 smaller 1 km² squares. The lines which divide them are referred to as grid lines. Each grid line is numbered. It is these numbers which we use to make grid references.

A grid reference is made up of the following:

    Letter
    Easting   **LEN**
    Northing

The Letter – always in blue – is the sub zone letter. It shows what part of the country it is in.

The Eastings are the vertical grid lines and they are numbered at the top and bottom of an OS map. They are called eastings because the number gets bigger as you go towards the east.

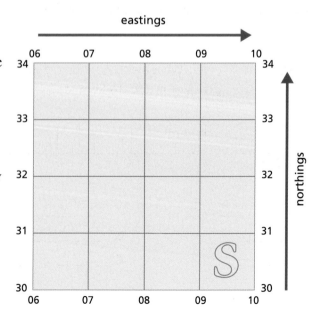

The Northings are the horizontal grid lines and they are numbered along the sides to the left and right. They are called northings because the numbers get bigger as you go towards the north.

Four-figure grid references

Four-figure grid references are used to locate full squares in which a feature is found, such as a lake or a village.

1. First you give the *letter* shown on the map.

2. Then you give the eastings number to the *left* of the square which the feature is in.

3. Then the northings number at the *bottom* of the square which the feature is in.

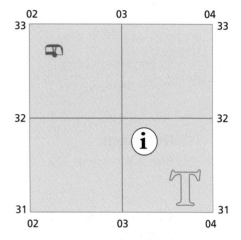

The four-figure grid reference for the caravan site is T 02 32.

Letter	→	T
Eastings	→	02
Northings	→	32

Six-figure grid references

A six-figure grid reference gives the exact location of a feature. Follow the exercises below to give six-figure grid references.

Eastings

Imagine this is a ruler. What are the numbers marked? The first two are done for you. (The ruler is marked in 1/10ths between whole numbers.)

X	1.5	A	_____
Y	3.0	B	_____
Z	_____	C	_____

Now the 1/10 marks have been taken out.
Give the reading for each number –
Do not put in the decimal point.

When giving grid references
you don't use **points**.

X	32 3	A	36 0
Y	_____	B	_____
Z	_____	C	_____

Northings

Give side readings. **Do not** put in the decimal point.

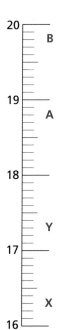

X _____ 16 3 _____

Y _____

A _____

B _____

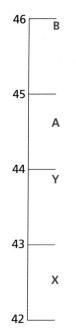

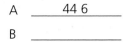

X _____

Y _____

A _____ 44 6 _____

B _____

Put the two together.

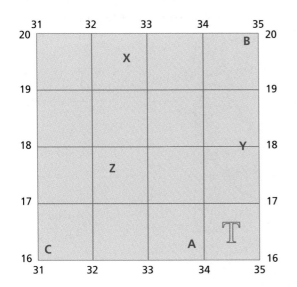

	Letter	Easting	Northing
X	T	32 7	19 6
Y	___	___	___
Z	___	___	___
A	T	33 8	16 3
B	___	___	___
C	___	___	___

Study the map of Killala (page 22) and answer the following questions.

1. Give the **four-figure** grid references for the following features:

		Letter	Easting	Northing
a.	Bone Rock	___	___	___
b.	Curraghfin Lough	___	___	___
c.	Trabaun	___	___	___
d.	Rinnaun Point	___	___	___

2. Give the **six-figure** grid references for the following features:

		Letter	Easting	Northing
e.	Post office in Killala	___	___	___
f.	Parking at Lackan Bay	___	___	___
g.	Round tower at Killala	___	___	___
h.	Castle at Rathfran Bay	___	___	___

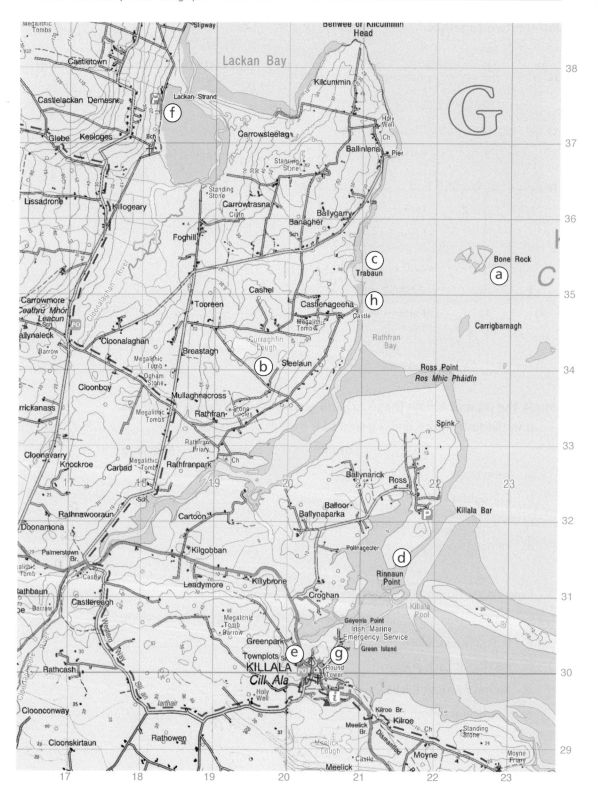

3. What **feature** is found at the following grid reference?

    G 202 366   Holy well   ☐   Stone circles   ☐

                     Standing stone   ☐   Parking   ☐

    What **feature** is found at the following grid reference?

    G 219 322   Post office   ☐   Parking   ☐

                     Barrow   ☐   Bone Rock   ☐

    What **feature** is found at the following grid reference?

    G 171 346   Post office   ☐   Trabaun   ☐

                     Round tower   ☐   Church   ☐

    What **feature** is located at the following grid reference?

    G 207 304   Green Island   ☐   Holy Well   ☐

                     Parking   ☐   Irish Marine   ☐

Chapter 5
Map symbols

A symbol is a drawing that stands for something shown on a map. **Symbols** are instead of words.

It would be hard to write down everything in detail on a map, so symbols are used to show where features are that would be of interest to us. They are shown in a *key* or *legend*. The meaning of each symbol is given in both Irish and English.

General features and boundaries

Foirgnimh le hais a chéile
Built up Area

Aerfort
Airport

Aerpháirc
Airfield

PO Oifig phoist
Post Office

Garda Síochána
Police

Stáisiún cumhachta (uisce)
Power Station (Hydro)

Stáisiún cumhachta
(breosla iontaiseach)
Power Station (Fossil)

Líne tarchurtha leictreachais
Electricity Transmission Line

A place where lots of people live, e.g. a town or a city.

Hydro: energy is created through falling water.

Fossil: energy is created by burning fossil fuels such as peat, coal and oil.

Crann
Mast

Eaglais no séipéal
Church or Chapel

Ardeaglais
Cathedral

Cuaille traintánaghta
Triangular Pillar

Trasnú cliathráin
Graticule Intersection

Siúlbealach le comharthaí;
gan comharthaí
Waymarked Walks; Unmarked

Bád fartha (feithiclí)
Ferry (Vehicle)

Bád fartha (paisinéirí)
Ferry (Passenger)

A pillar which shows exact height at that point.

Teorainn idirnáisiúnta
International Boundary

Teorainn chontae
County Boundary

Páirc Náisiúnta
National Park

Páirc Foraoise
Forest Park

Seilbh de chuid an Aire Chosanta
Dept. of Defence Property

Foraois bhuaircíneach
Coniferous Plantation

Coill nádúrtha
Natural Woodland

Foraois mheasctha
Mixed Woodland

Look carefully at the key and draw out the symbols for the following features:

Garda station

Church

Power station (fossil)

Natural woodland

Airport

Mast

There are three types of forest shown on the key on page 24. Say what they are, draw the symbol for each and find out what types of tree may grow in them.

Forest		Tree types
1. _____		_____
2. _____		_____
3. _____		_____

Tourism symbols

Ordnance Survey maps are important to tourists visiting the country. They can show what services the tourist can use and what activities they can do.

Look at the Tourist Information symbols and answer the questions below.

Eolas Turasóireachta
Tourist Information

- Láithreán carbhán (idirthurais)
  Caravan site (transit)
- Brú An Óige / Neamhspleách
  Hostel An Óige / Independent
- **P** Ionad pairceála
  Parking
- Láithreán picnicí
  Picnic site
- **C** Teilefón Poiblí
  Public Telephone
- Láithreán campála
  Camping site

- **i** Ionad eolais turasóireachta
  (ar oscailt ar feadh na bliana)
  Tourist Information centre
  (regular opening)
- *i* Ionad eolais turasóireachta
  (ar oscailt le linn an tséasúir)
  Tourist Information centre
  (restricted opening)
- Ionad dearctha
  Viewpoint
- A T An Taisce
  National Trust
- Tearmann Dúlra
  Nature Reserve
- 9 18 Galfchúrsa, machaire galif
  Golf Course or Links

1. What information is shown by these symbols?

   a) [⊓] _____   c) [☀] _____

   b) [🏠] _____   d) [*C*] _____

2. There are symbols for three types of place to stay; **accommodation**.
   Draw the three symbols and say what each means.

   a) [   ] _____

   b) [   ] _____

   c) [   ] _____

   Tourist information centres give information about local attractions, services, opening hours and costs.

3. There are two tourist information centres. What is the difference between the two?

   i _____

   i _____

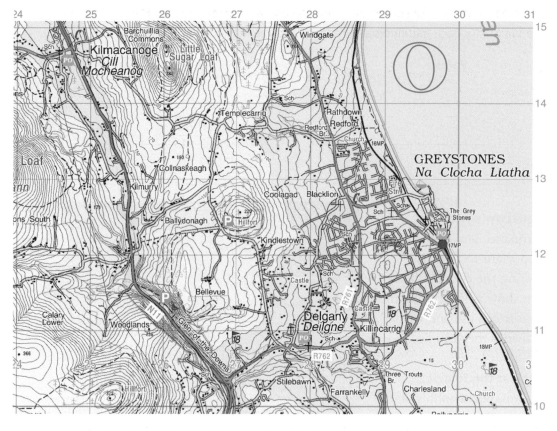

Study the map and answer the questions below.

1. How many churches are there in Greystones? _____

2. To the north-west of Greystones there is a small built-up area.

   Name the area. _____

   There are three symbols in this built-up area: draw each one and say what it means.

   a) [   ] _____

   b) [   ] _____

   c) [   ] _____

3. What type of woodland is located at **O 27 14**?

   Coniferous ☐   Natural ☐   Mixed ☐

4. At which of the following grid references will you find a **Garda station**?

   O 126 292 ☐   O 284 134 ☐   O 296 126 ☐   O 306 136 ☐

5. What **feature** is located at the following grid reference? **O 262 114**

   Parking ☐   Nature reserve ☐   Post office ☐   Golf course ☐

6. In the boxes provided, match each letter in column X with the number of its pair in column Y. One pair is completed for you.

X				Y					
	A	Golf course			1	O 279 109		A	3
	B	Picnic site			2	O 262 115		B	
	C	Public telephone			3	O 292 113		C	
	D	Parking			4	O 248 149		D	
	E	Post office			5	O 269 124		E	

Revision – Greystones map extract

1. In what direction from the post office in Kilmacanoge **(O 246 147)** is the post office in Delgany **(O 279 109)**?

   South-east ☐   South-west ☐   North-east ☐   North ☐

2. In what direction from the post office in Delgany **(O 279 109)** is the post office in Greystones?

   South-east ☐   North-west ☐   North ☐   North-east ☐

3. In what direction are you travelling along the N11 from the Glen of the Downs **(O 26 10)** to Kilmacanoge **(O 24 14)**?

   _____

4. Measure the distance, in kilometres, between the post office in Kilmacanoge **(O 246 147)** to the post office in Delgany **(O 279 109)**.

   4.9 km ☐   3.5 km ☐   5.6 km ☐   4.2 km ☐

5. What is the distance, in kilometres, along the N11 road from its junction with the R762 **(O 268 104)** to the post office in Kilmacanoge **(O 246 147)**?

   _____

6. The area (in square kilometres) shown on this map is about

   25 km² ☐   12 km² ☐   35 km² ☐   24 km² ☐

7. What is the approximate area (in square kilometres) of the sea to the east of Greystones?

   _____

Map symbols

Look at the symbols below and find their meaning in the word search,

e.g. 1. ⊕ = Airport

M	N	Q	D	D	F	R	L	C	G	A	A	E	T	M	T	L
C	O	L	U	E	V	X	A	G	W	G	C	E	O	F	E	A
M	I	P	A	R	O	R	P	O	A	I	M	T	U	A	L	N
G	T	H	W	N	A	G	O	L	F	C	O	U	R	S	E	O
R	A	C	O	V	O	D	J	F	J	P	S	O	I	P	P	I
G	L	V	A	S	L	I	O	R	U	D	P	H	S	R	H	T
Z	U	N	I	A	T	T	G	T	B	G	D	X	T	O	O	A
D	G	G	N	E	S	E	L	E	C	H	U	R	C	H	N	N
M	N	D	N	O	W	I	L	C	R	H	C	A	E	B	E	Q
Y	A	W	P	I	U	P	Y	A	W	R	O	T	O	M	E	Q
A	I	Y	A	B	K	G	O	A	I	R	P	O	R	T	D	S
W	R	E	G	L	N	R	G	I	T	G	N	I	P	M	A	C
L	T	N	E	I	K	A	A	H	N	P	U	H	I	L	Z	L
I	K	A	T	K	R	W	P	P	X	T	B	D	C	G	C	I
A	C	A	M	D	A	L	A	U	R	G	X	H	N	U	A	I
R	O	A	A	R	Q	L	E	Y	Q	S	X	B	I	W	I	D
B	I	J	F	D	K	C	H	E	Q	P	S	N	C	C	Z	J

1. ⊕ _____

2.  🗺 b_____u_____ area

3. † _____

4. ⬆ _____

5. ▬▬▬ National or regional road?

_____

6. PO _____

7. ⟳ _____

8. � _____

9. ⌣ _____

10. ⌂ _____

11. ★ G_____ Station

12. ⬭ _____

13. P _____

14. —•— R_____ station

15. ℹ T_____ centre

16. - - - W_____ way

17. ⬦ _____

18. ⬠ _____

19. ⛳₁₈ _____

20. ⬥ _____

21. ⊼ _____

22. ▬▬▬ National or regional road?

_____

23. △ T_____ pillar

24. ⬭ Mixed w_____

Chapter 6
Drawing sketch maps

You have been asked to draw a sketch map of the North County Dublin area as shown on the Ordnance Survey map on page 16. You are to mark and identify:

- a railway line
- two named roads
- a beach
- a golf course
- one town.

So how do you go about drawing your sketch map?

Step 1

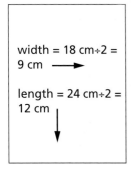

width = 18 cm÷2 = 9 cm →

length = 24 cm÷2 = 12 cm ↓

Draw frame

Draw a frame for your sketch map. It is to be smaller but of the same shape as the OS map. A handy guide is to draw it to quarter the size (measure length and width of the OS map) and divide by 2.

Step 2

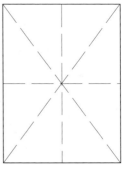

Draw grid lines

Draw in guidelines lightly on both the sketch and the OS map to help you place features.

Step 3

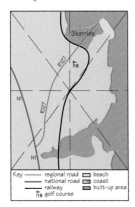

Draw and name features

Draw in the coastline (if any) and any features you have been asked to mark. After drawing in the features you must name them. This is called *identifying* the features. Use a basic key, if you wish, to help you.

Step 4

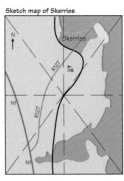

Title and direction arrow

Give your sketch map a title (or name) and north direction arrow.

Tips

- Always use pencil and ruler.
- Always label or name (identify) your features (most marks are lost by students not labelling or naming the feature they have drawn).
- Only draw what you have been asked to in the question.
- Draw your towns to the same shape as the outline of the grey built-up area.

Marking ✓

Total: 12 marks

2 marks for each feature:

1 mark for showing + 1 mark for naming

1 mark for frame

1 mark for title or direction arrow.

(Exercises on sketch maps are at the back of this book.)

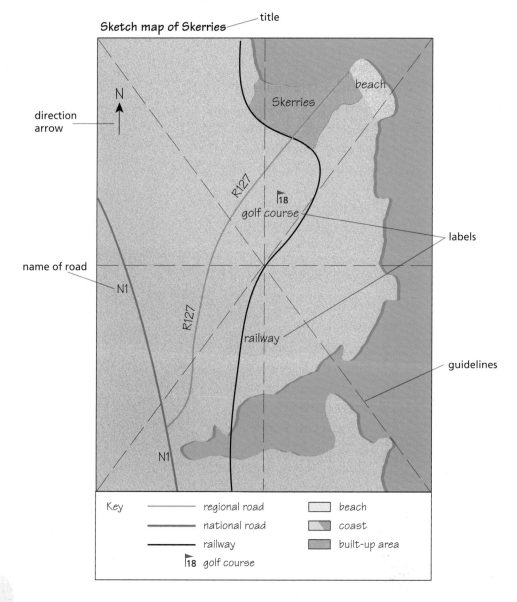

Chapter 7
Relief on Ordnance Survey maps

Relief is to do with the shape and height of the earth's surface.
Height is shown on an OS map in four main ways.

Colour
Shading changes to show height. Green shows
lowland and changes to brown. The higher you go,
the darker the colour.

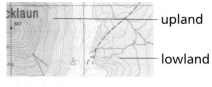

upland

lowland

Contour lines
Contour lines join places of the same height. They are
spaced out 10 m apart with the 50 m line being a little
heavier. The numbers get bigger the higher you go.

contour
lines

Spot height
A spot with a number beside it shows the exact
height at that point. Here it is 552 m above sea level.

spot
height

Triangulation pillar
This is shown by a triangle with a number beside it.
It shows the exact height. At this point there is a
pillar with brass grooves which held instruments
which were used to map the landscape in the past.

triangulation
pillar

Draw in the contour lines by joining the places of equal height.

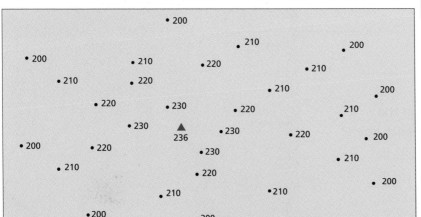

Nephin Beg

On this map extract the spot heights have been taken out.
Match up the spot heights A–E.

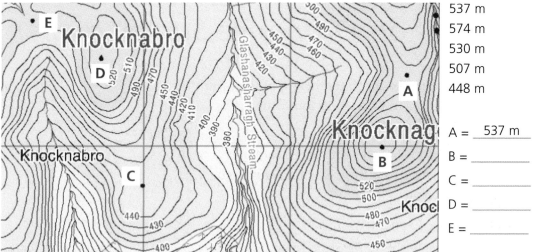

537 m
574 m
530 m
507 m
448 m

A = ___537 m___

B = _____

C = _____

D = _____

E = _____

Match up the words in the list with their descriptions below.

● colour   ● contour lines   ● spot height   ● triangulation pillar

1. Shading that goes darker to show height   _____

2. A triangle with a number beside it that shows exact height   _____

3. Lines that join places of equal height   _____

4. A spot with a number beside it that shows exact height   _____

Use the words to label the
map correctly.

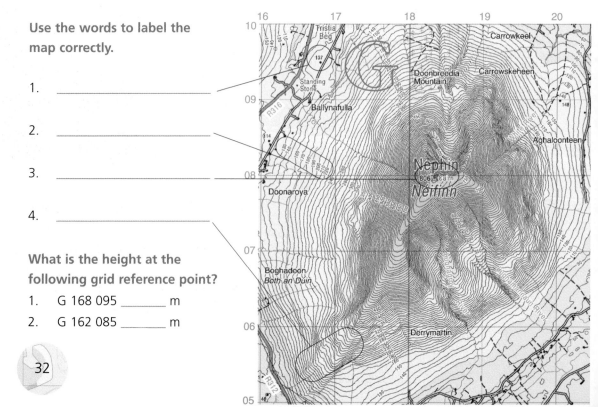

1. _____

2. _____

3. _____

4. _____

What is the height at the
following grid reference point?

1. G 168 095 _____ m

2. G 162 085 _____ m

The difference in height between G 168 095 and G 184 079 (triangulation pillar) is:

512 m ☐   669 m ☐   418 m ☐   704 m ☐

Showing slope

The steepness of slopes is shown by how close the contour lines are together. The closer the contours, the steeper the slope.

B

This is an area in the Sheeffry Mountains (A). It has been enlarged in diagram B. If you were walking from X to Y you would be climbing upwards and the slope would be getting steeper as you go. How do you know this?

- The colour is changing from green to brown.
- Contour lines are getting closer.

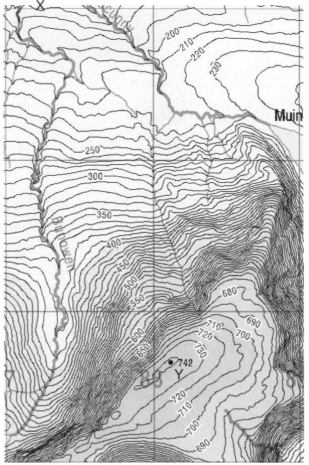

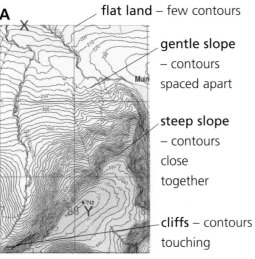

A

flat land – few contours

gentle slope – contours spaced apart

steep slope – contours close together

cliffs – contours touching

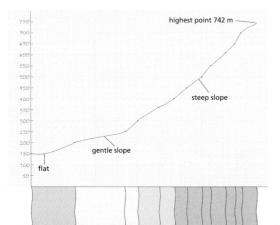

The contour lines have been drawn onto a graph in a *cross section* so you can see what the slope may look like in reality.

It starts off flat or with a gentle slope, and as the contours get closer the slope gets steeper.

33

Look at the map below of the Sheeffry Hills. At A–D say what type of slope you think is there and give two reasons for your answer.

● flat land   ● gentle slope   ● steep slope   ● cliffs

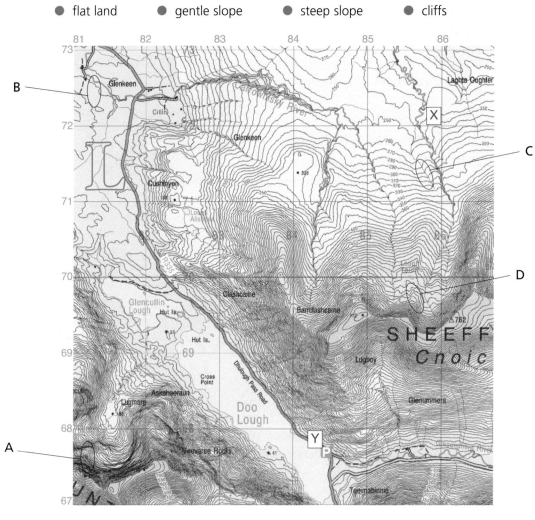

A. **L 81 67**   Type of slope: Cliffs
   Explanation: 1. **Contours** are nearly touching.
                   2. **Colour** is dark brown-black.

B. **L 81 72**   Type of slope: _____
   Explanation: 1. _____
                   2. _____

C. **L 85 71**   Type of slope: _____
   Explanation: 1. _____
                   2. _____

D. **L 85 69**   Type of slope: _____
   Explanation: 1. _____
                   2. _____

If you were to climb this peak to Barrclashcame at **L 849 695** which would be steepest?

To climb from the NE at X ☐ or

To climb from the SW at Y ☐

Give reasons for your choice: _____

_____

Some types of slope

Slopes may also take different shapes and it is important to know the different types of slope.

1. Even slope:

There is an even space between the contours.

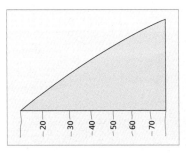
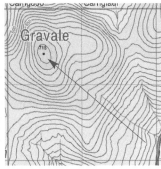

2. Concave slope:

Gentle near the base (widely spaced contours), steep near the top (close contours).

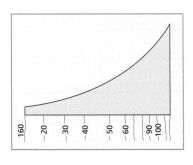

Tip
To help you remember the shape: goes <u>in</u> like a cave – con<u>cave</u>

3. Convex slope:

Steep near the base (close contours), less steep near the top (widely spaced contours).

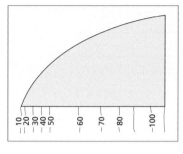 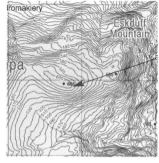 

4. Compound slope:

Part is concave and part is convex.

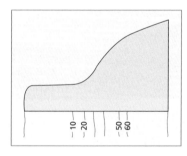 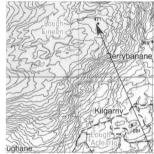 

Exam-type questions

● even slope ● concave slope ● convex slope ● compound slope

1. Label each of the diagrams A to D with the correct type of slope.

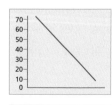 A. _____

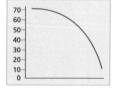 B. _____

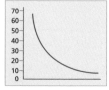 C. _____

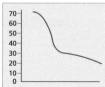 D. _____

2. This diagram shows what type of slope?   *(tick box)*

   Even   ☐

   Concave   ☐

   Convex   ☐

   Compound   ☐

3. This diagram shows what type of slope?   *(tick box)*

   Even   ☐

   Concave   ☐

   Convex   ☐

   Compound   ☐

4. This diagram shows what type of slope?   *(tick box)*

   Even   ☐

   Concave   ☐

   Convex   ☐

   Compound   ☐

5. What type of slope is being shown from A to B? and C to D?

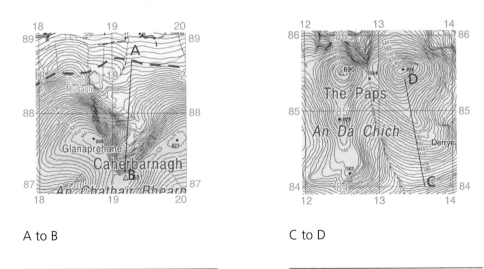

A to B

_____

C to D

_____

Cross sections

When you look at a mountainous area on an Ordnance Survey map, it can be hard to imagine what shape the mountains take. A cross section of the area helps you to do just that.

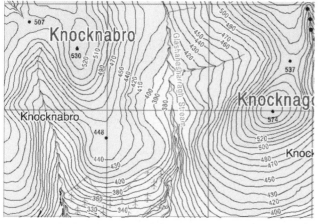

Here the map section has been made bigger to show clearly how to draw a cross section. We are going to do a cross section from the spot height at Knocknabro 530 m **A** to the spot height at Knocknagowan 574 m **B**.

1. Draw a line between the two points you wish to measure (A–B).

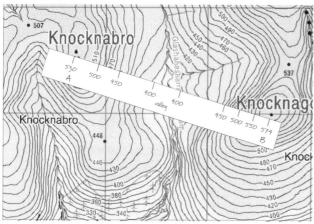

2. Take a piece of paper and line up the straight edge with the A–B line. Mark on the paper A and B and their heights. Mark where the contour lines cut the paper at 50 m intervals and note the heights.

   Handy hint: Contour lines are spaced at 10 m but the 50 m lines are slightly heavier.

3. Draw a graph to show this information. The horizontal axis is the same length from A to B. The vertical axis is drawn at _each end_ and the height goes in equal intervals of 50 m from 0 upwards.

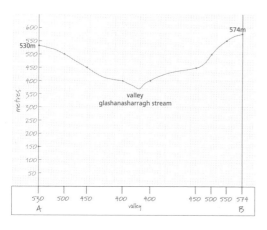

4. Place your A–B paper on the vertical axis and mark each contour directly above it and across from the correct height.

5. Join the points together in a smooth curve.

Over to you

Draw a cross section of the area from Luggala, spot height 595 m to Knocknacloghoge in the south, spot height 534 m.

Show this information on the graph below.

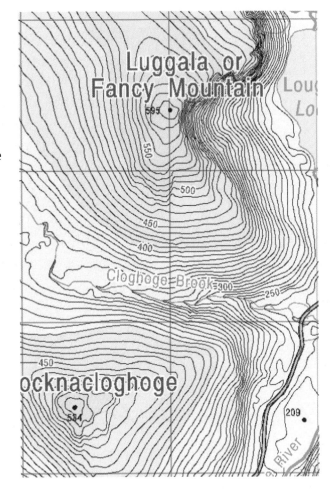

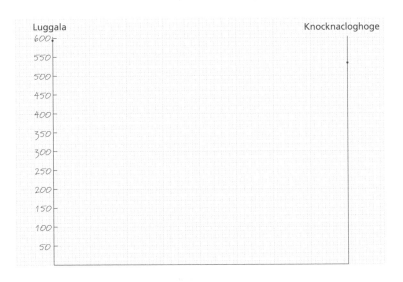

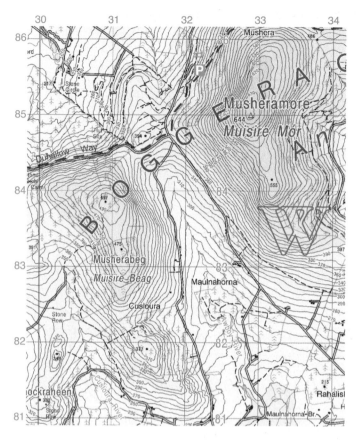

Now try it with a 1:50,000 OS map.

Draw a cross section of the area from Musheramore **W 328 850** to Musherabeg **W 312 833**.

Now represent the information on a graph.

Study the map extract on page 42 and answer the following questions:

1. List the four ways you can tell height on this map.
   a. _____   b. _____
   c. _____   d. _____

2. The height at the spot height at **F 996 017** is
   538 m ☐   341 m ☐   588 m ☐   349 m ☐

3. The highest point shown on this map is _____ m, found at _____ (grid ref).

4. The difference in height between **G 004 044** (Mount Eagle) and **G 025 050**
   (Birreencorragh) is
   147 m ☐   358 m ☐   271 m ☐   131 m ☐

5. Imagine you have climbed from the shore of Bunaveela Lough F 992 090 to the
   triangulation pillar at **G 025 050**. What height would you have climbed?
   578 m ☐   497 m ☐   568 m ☐   388 m   ☐

6. Steepness of slope:
   ● flat land   ● gentle slope   ● steep slope   ● cliffs
   What is the steepness of slope at the following locations?
   G 02 05   _____
   G 03 08   _____
   G 04 03   _____

7. If you were to climb the peak at Knockaffertagh (**G 047 049**) would it be less
   steep to climb from the north-east or from the south-west?
   It would be less steep to climb from the _____
   Explain briefly how you would know: _____
   _____

8. Types of slope:
   ● even   ● convex   ● concave   ● compound
   What types of slope are at the following locations?
   G 03 03   _____
   G 04 05   _____

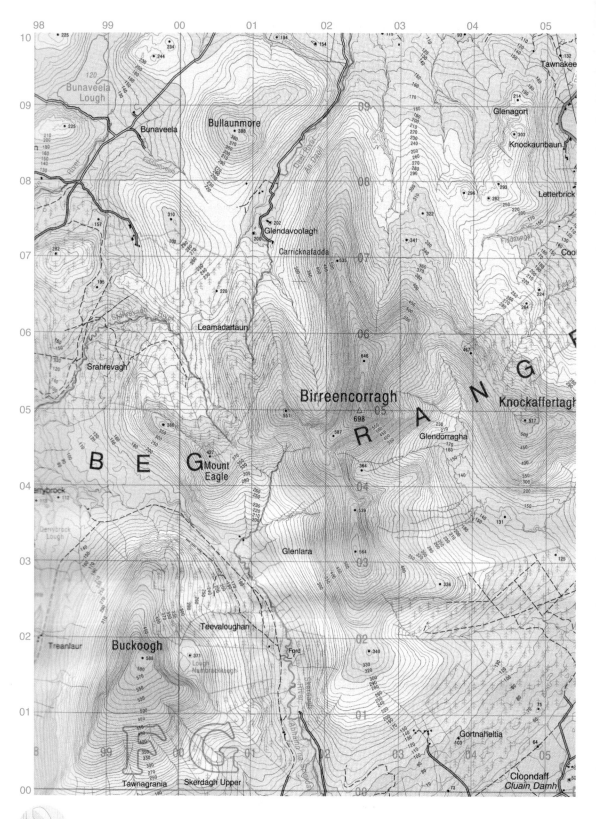

Shape and height of the earth's surface

Mountain: steep-sided landform over 400 m in height
Hill: steep-sided landform under 400 m in height
Ridge: a long narrow area of high land
Col: a gap between two higher points of land
Spur: a tongue of high land that sticks out
Valley: a narrow dip, which may have a river or lake in it

col (dip)   mountain

ridge (long area of high land)

spur (tongue of land)

valley (with lake in it)

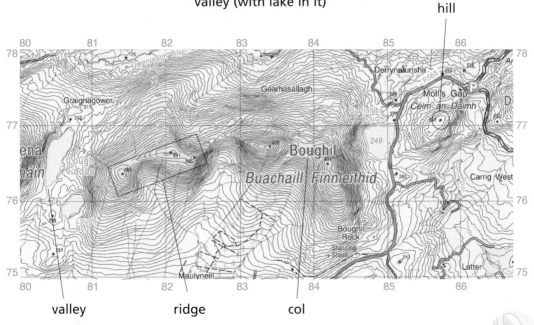

hill

valley   ridge   col

Relief on OS maps

Look at the map and diagrams below, which are to do with relief on OS maps, and say what each one shows.

Shapes of slopes: what shape of slope is shown here?

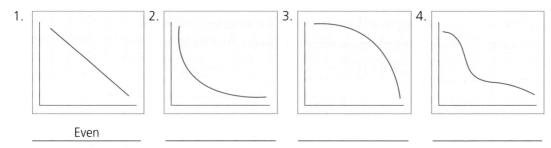

1. _____Even_____   2. _____   3. _____   4. _____

What relief features are shown here?

10. gentle slope   15. S_____ slope   14. V_____   13. T_____ pillar

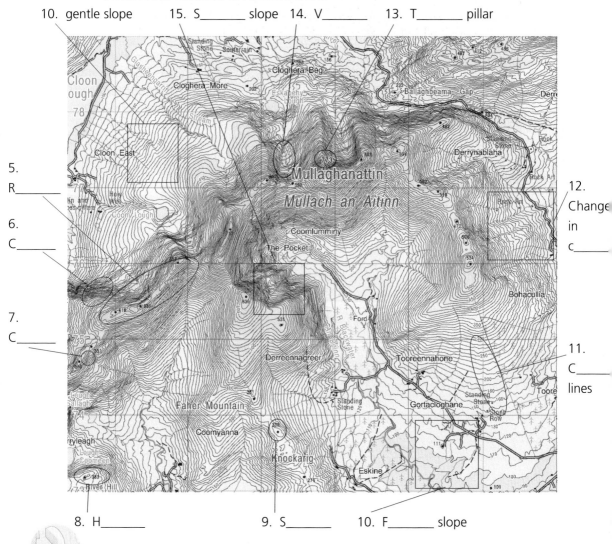

5. R_____

6. C_____

7. C_____

12. Change in c_____

11. C_____ lines

8. H_____   9. S_____   10. F_____ slope

Find the solutions in the word search below.

S	R	U	O	T	N	O	C	T	G	H	F	E	H	P
D	U	E	W	A	C	N	E	R	J	E	V	N	B	E
V	N	S	P	O	Z	G	I	I	A	A	N	D	V	E
O	F	U	N	O	D	G	W	A	C	Q	T	T	Q	T
W	N	V	O	I	L	T	X	N	L	H	M	M	L	S
M	E	A	R	P	O	S	O	G	I	I	L	I	P	E
X	Q	M	O	T	M	C	D	U	F	L	V	O	F	U
Y	E	L	L	A	V	O	J	L	F	L	T	N	O	C
K	C	X	O	M	L	D	C	A	S	H	K	I	Y	R
E	Y	F	L	A	T	N	S	T	E	W	F	A	I	G
W	V	N	Y	U	L	P	O	I	W	Y	J	T	B	A
F	V	E	Y	P	U	V	G	O	A	J	T	N	O	P
V	B	Q	N	R	L	H	D	N	N	H	V	U	H	N
E	M	O	M	J	T	E	C	G	E	O	O	O	D	U
L	O	C	C	C	O	L	O	U	R	C	B	M	O	K

Drainage on OS maps

Drainage is the way in which water is taken from the land surface naturally, such as rivers, lakes and marshes.

An area which is poorly drained has too much surface water, like many lakes or marshes.

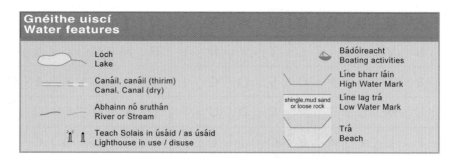

Gnéithe uiscí
Water features

Loch / Lake	Bádóireacht / Boating activities
Canáil, canáil (thirim) / Canal, Canal (dry)	Líne bharr láin / High Water Mark
Abhainn nó sruthán / River or Stream	shingle,mud sand or loose rock — Líne lag trá / Low Water Mark
Teach Solais in úsáid / as úsáid / Lighthouse in use / disuse	Trá / Beach

1. _____   2. _____   3. _____

5.
_____

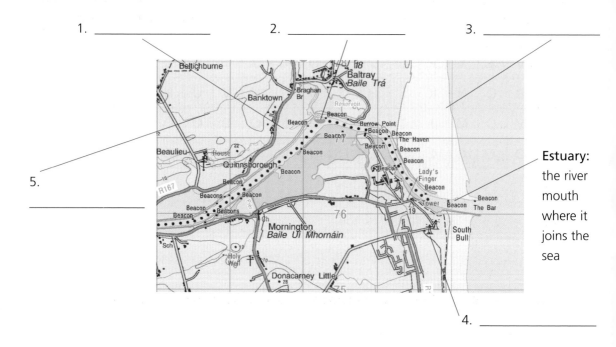

Estuary: the river mouth where it joins the sea

4. _____

Label the map extract with the following features:

river / stream   beach   Lake

boating activities   lighthouse

Keywords

Communications	Route focus
Function	Antiquities
Potential	Density of settlement

river — roads

Communications: Ways to allow transport, such as roads, rivers, railways and canals.

Route focus: A place where roads lead to and seem to meet (or *converge*).

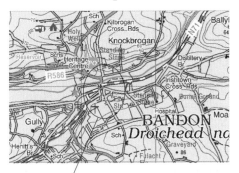

Places of importance from the past

Antiquities: Places of historical importance. Shown in red writing on a map.

Roads converging

Bandon is a **route focus**.

Function: The services and activities that benefit the people who live there or in the surrounding areas.

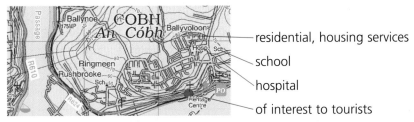

residential, housing services

school

hospital

of interest to tourists

Potential: Anything that might be possible

Tourist potential: How an area might grow and develop to attract tourists.

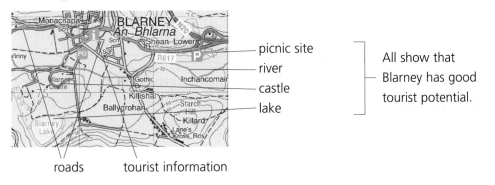

picnic site

river

castle

lake

All show that Blarney has good tourist potential.

roads   tourist information

Density of settlement: Looks at the number of people living in a given area.

High density
of settlement

Low density
of settlement

Keywords

S	J	K	I	Y	T	I	S	O	T	U	D	Z	C	T
S	E	I	T	I	U	Q	I	T	N	A	M	O	F	N
T	S	I	R	U	O	T	R	S	S	T	M	E	U	E
W	K	Y	T	T	H	O	E	U	G	M	G	T	N	M
N	F	A	O	I	P	R	C	Y	U	Y	B	U	C	E
F	Y	E	N	S	V	O	C	N	T	Q	O	O	T	L
Z	I	W	N	I	F	I	I	O	E	I	K	R	I	T
J	C	A	C	V	S	C	T	Y	N	C	S	T	O	T
L	R	E	N	M	A	Q	V	C	H	V	G	N	N	E
T	S	P	O	T	E	N	T	I	A	L	E	B	E	S
O	O	O	I	D	K	T	S	Q	R	I	J	R	X	D
H	H	O	F	P	T	L	O	H	R	T	M	J	G	I
T	N	A	F	P	P	R	V	A	X	I	J	J	H	E
S	A	C	A	U	I	U	E	V	Z	Y	Q	C	M	O
O	E	E	F	S	T	N	B	U	U	P	L	D	L	W

activities	antiquities	communications	converge	density
focus	function	potential	route	services
settlement	tourist	transport		

Keywords

Across

1. Ways to allow transportation
4. To meet or join up
5. Where roads seem to meet or join
6. The services and activities that benefit the people
7. _____ settlement: the amount of people living in an area

Down

2. Places of importance from the past
3. Anything that might grow or develop has _____

Communications here means transport such as roads, rivers, railways and canals. The symbols for roads and railways are given below.

Slip roads are used to exit and join onto motorways.

Motorways are designed to provide faster journey times with greater safety. They have no traffic lights. The speed limit is 70 mph.

Dual carriageways have two lanes for each direction of traffic.

These roads connect to major roads, and connect rural areas (countryside) to larger towns and villages.

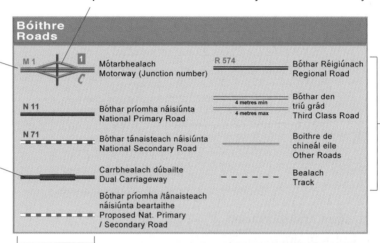

Bóithre Roads

M 1 1 C	Mótarbhealach Motorway (Junction number)
N 11	Bóthar príomha náisiúnta National Primary Road
N 71	Bóthar tánaisteach náisiúnta National Secondary Road
	Carrbhealach dúbailte Dual Carriageway
	Bóthar príomha /tánaisteach náisiúnta beartaithe Proposed Nat. Primary / Secondary Road
R 574	Bóthar Réigiúnach Regional Road
4 metres min / 4 metres max	Bóthar den triú grád Third Class Road
	Boithre de chineál eile Other Roads
– – – – –	Bealach Track

These roads connect main towns.

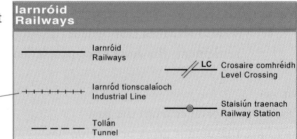

Iarnróid Railways

———	Iarnróid Railways
+++++++++	Iarnród tionscalaíoch Industrial Line
– – – –	Tollán Tunnel
// LC	Crosaire comhréidh Level Crossing
——●—	Staisiún traenach Railway Station

Used to transport raw materials and goods.

Look at the symbols and the colours of the roads on the Ordnance Survey keys.

Colour in the roads on the map of Castleban correctly according to the labels.

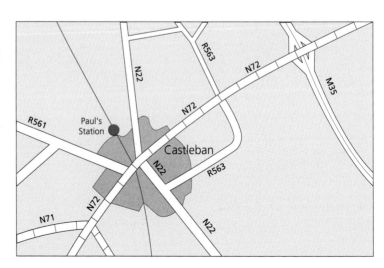

The building of roads is influenced by the landscape.
Roads will *avoid* upland, flood plains and poorly drained land.

Avoid upland

Why?   It is difficult and expensive to build on steep slopes. Not many
people live upland because of poor weather conditions, thin soil.
(*Low density* of population.)

Avoid flood plains and poorly drained lands (areas with a lot of surface water)

Why?   To avoid flooding which will cause disruption to traffic and
damage to roads.

So where are roads built?

Route focus –
where roads lead
to and seem to
meet up

- Low-lying, flat or gently sloping land
- Along the base (bottom) of mountains or through gaps, valleys
- Areas where a lot of people live (*high density* of population) to
allow access.

staying away from
poorly drained land

high population density (a lot
of people live here; built up)

Millstreet is the
route focus

low-lying, flat or
gently sloping land

road
makes its
way
around
base of
mountain

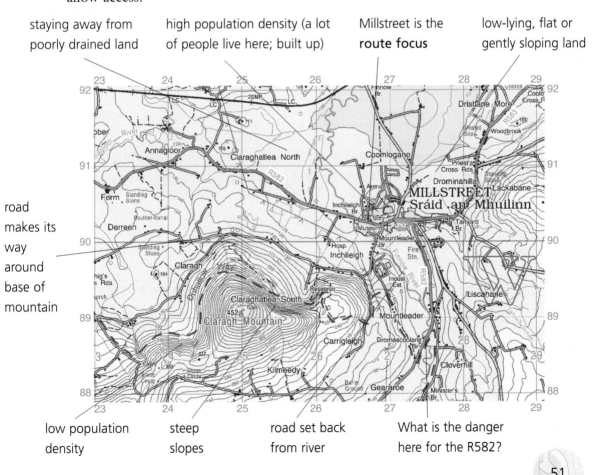

low population
density

steep
slopes

road set back
from river

What is the danger
here for the R582?

Sample question

Describe how the R582 road has been influenced by the landscape.

You need to write at least three points to answer a question fully.
Each point must have your statement, location and a development which explains your answer further. The magnifying glass shows the layout of points.

Sample answer

The R582 has been influenced by the landscape around it.

 It avoids the steep slopes of Claragh Mountain, for example, at **W 25 89**. This is because it is difficult and expensive to build roads on steep slopes.

It avoids the flood plain of the Finnow River, as can be seen at **W 27 89**, to prevent flooding, which would cause damage and disruption. The road instead runs along low-lying gently sloping land, for example at **W 25 90**, and around the base of the Claragh Mountain taking the easiest route.

Point 1. Breakdown

statement   location

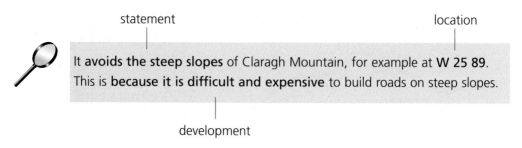 It **avoids the steep slopes** of Claragh Mountain, for example at **W 25 89**. This is **because it is difficult and expensive** to build roads on steep slopes.

development

These are the three parts for which marks are given and they must be included in your answer.

Describe how the N22 road has been influenced by the landscape.

Finish the answer below, try to make three points in all.

Road runs through **valley** of Flesk River.

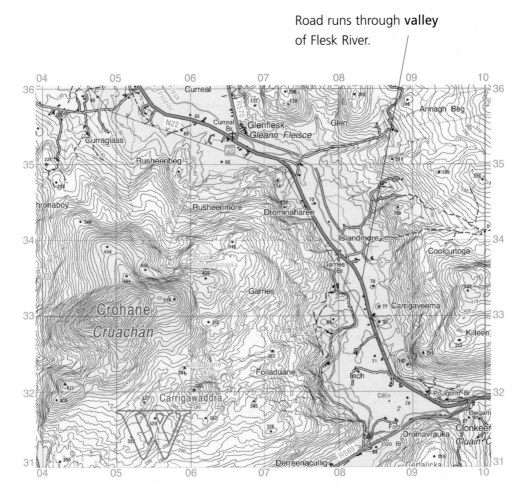

The building of the N22 has been influenced by the landscape around it.

Point 1.

It avoids _____ as can be seen at _____

because _____

Point 2.

_____

_____

Point 3.

_____

_____

Chapter 9
Tourism on Ordnance Survey maps

Ordnance Survey maps can tell you a lot about the tourist potential of an area. Imagine you are going to organise a week-long holiday in Galway. What decisions would you need to make?

Activities: What could you see and do when you get there?
Accommodation: Where are you going to stay?
Services: What facilities will you use on your stay?
Transport: How you are going to get there?

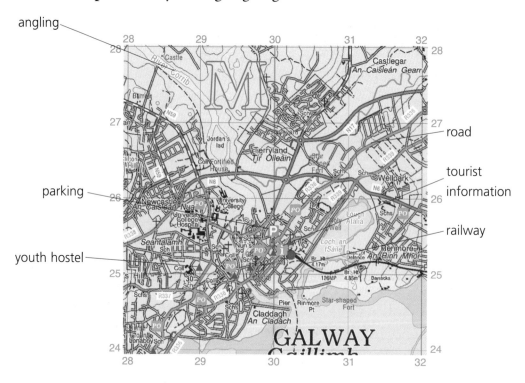

angling

parking

youth hostel

road

tourist information

railway

Factors to take into account when looking at tourist potential

Transport/access

Areas which are trying to attract tourists should have a good transport network. It should be easy for the tourist to get there and to travel about (access). Areas which are easily *accessible* will have good road networks (national routeways). They may also have railways and airports nearby.

Services

Services are facilities available which the tourist may use to help make their stay easier and more enjoyable.

There are a lot of services available for the tourist at Tramore.

List five, draw the symbol for each and give the grid reference.

1. Picnic site   ⊓   S 589 024

2. _____   ☐   _____

3. _____   ☐   _____

4. _____   ☐   _____

5. _____   ☐   _____

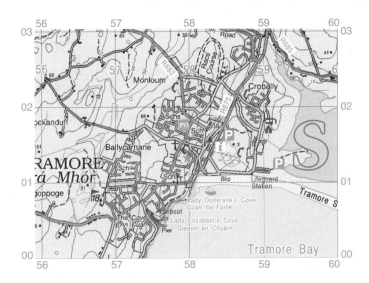

Built-up areas like Tramore and Galway will have a lot more to offer the tourist than is marked on the map. It would be impossible to mark in all the restaurants, banks, bars, etc. that are probably there. There may also be other choices of *accommodation* such as B&Bs and hotels.

Activities

Ireland can offer many activities and attractions for tourists.

* *Coastal areas:* Irish coastal towns such as Tramore provide a lot of activities. There are boating activities, fishing, beaches for swimming, walks and picnics.

* *Rivers, canals, lakes:* waterways give opportunities for walks and picnics on the banks, or for fishing and boating activities.

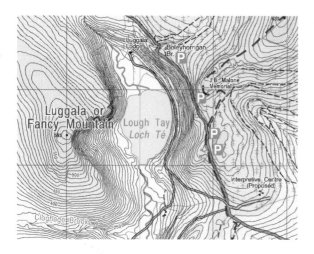

- *Forests* may also have walkways (— — —) or tracks (— — —) marked in them. Picnic sites may be available.

- *Mountains* are of interest to hill walkers or climbers and give excellent views.

- *Antiquities* are places of historical importance and may be of great interest to the tourist. Antiquities on a map are shown using red writing. Some sites are developed for the tourist market. Here the site of the Battle of the Boyne has parking, picnic areas, good access with a national routeway and the extra activity of golfing.

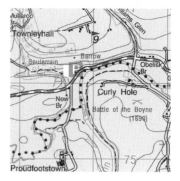

Other tourist activities can include golfing, racecourses and nature reserves.

Look at the Ordnance Survey map of the Blessington area. It has a lot of tourist potential with many attractions.

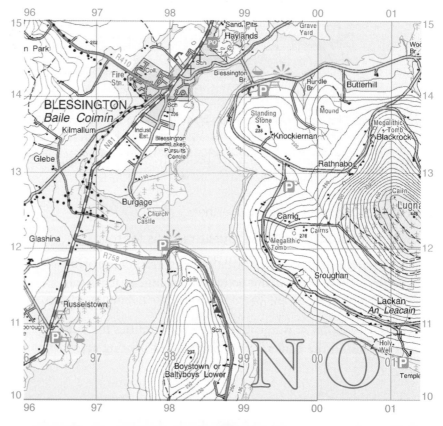

Imagine you work for Bord Fáilte. Recommend two activities for each type of tourist listed below, based on map evidence only. Name the activity or attraction. Describe what you could do there and give the location with a grid reference.

Only answer with the information on the map in front of you, even though you may live in the area and know what is there.

Sightseer

1. **Viewpoint:** views of the lakes and the mountain to the east. There is also parking and a picnic site. It is located at **N 981 122**.

2. **Church and Castle:** historical sites to visit and learn about the area's past. **N 97 12**.

Outdoor type

1. _____
   _____

2. _____
   _____

Family

1. _____
   _____

2. _____
   _____

Look at the map of Killarney on page 114.
Imagine you work for Bord Fáilte and you have to draw up a tourist brochure for the area to go with the map extract.

Give information on:
- How to get there
- Where to stay
- Attractions and activities
  1. for families
  2. for those interested in outdoor activities
  3. for historians
- Services available.

1. Imagine you are on holidays in Tramore. Write a postcard to a friend
    and on it list *four* activities or attractions that can be seen on the map
    on page 55.

Exam question

Marking ✔
Marking: 8 marks (2 marks x 4) 2 marks for each activity or attraction listed.

Tips
*   Be careful of the differences between services and activities or attractions.
    Activities and attractions bring people or 'attract' them to an area. Services
    are the facilities they might need or use, e.g. parking is not an attraction but
    a service!
*   Don't just depend on features such as mountains, rivers and lakes – look at
    the landscape around and activities written on the map, such as race courses.

2. Imagine you are on holidays in Blessington. Write a postcard to a friend
    and on it list *four* activities or attractions that can be seen on the map
    on page 56.

3. **What evidence is on the map to suggest that Tramore (page 55) is a tourist resort?**

Exam question

Marking ✔
State evidence: 2 marks, location: 1 mark, development: 1 mark.

Tip
Roads and accessibility are not accepted as evidence.

First evidence

evidence / statement

Tramore is a highly developed tourist resort as can be seen from the map. It has provided **accommodation** for tourists with two caravan and camping sites, one located at **S 59 01**, and a hostel in the town centre at **S 584 016**. The town probably has other types of accommodation such as hotels and B&Bs. This shows that Tramore **gets a large number of tourists who need accommodation.**

location

development

Complete with two more points of evidence.

Hints:
- Services
- Attractions

_____

_____

_____

_____

Chapter 10
Place names

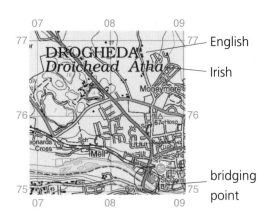

English

Irish

bridging
point

Place names can tell us a lot about the history of an area and its development (its growth over the years). The Irish name of a town which is given in *italics* beneath the English can show us where the name came from.

droichead = bridge
atha = crossing point

Drogheda may have developed or grown at this place because of the bridging point over the river.

Below is a list of the most common Irish words used in place names:

sliabh (slieve)	mountain	beag (beg)	small
cnoc (knock)	hill	in (een)	little
gleann (glen)	valley/glen	ard	high
ath	ford	dubh (duff)	black
lough	lake	sean	old
baile (bally)	small settlement	rua (roe)	red/brown
cill (kil)	church	dun	
ross	wood	rath	fort
mainistir (monaster)	monastery	cashel	
mor (more)	large		

Where do you think these place names came from?
1. Newbridge
2. Kilcullen
3. Monasterevin
4. Glenroe
5. Raheens
6. Rathmore

Tip
Place names may help you answer a question on why a town developed at a location.

You may have noticed small red writing on the Ordnance Survey maps that you have been studying. This red writing shows that there are antiquities there. Antiquities are sites of historical importance such as *standing stones* and *castles*.

Looking at these antiquities can help you to understand the development of a town or why our ancestors chose to settle where they did. This can be seen in place names.

7000 BC meso = middle lithos = stone	**Mesolithic Age** hunter-gatherers Mount Sandel flint	People lived near *water* for drinking, cooking, food supply and transport. Located on *hilltops* for defence	Not much evidence as they moved about. *Midden*: heaps of shells found in sand on seashores (water = lakeshores, riversides, estuaries)
4000 BC neo = new lithos = stone	**Neolithic Age** farmers Lough Gur	Cleared *forests* for farming. Examples found at Brownshill, Carlow e.g. Newgrange	*Megalithic tombs* provided the main evidence. Examples: *Dolmen*: a large copstone on top of two or three upright stones with a burial chamber underneath. *Passage tombs*: long passage which led to burial chambers covered by earth or stones.
1400 BC	**Bronze Age**	Some located *copper mines* copper + tin = bronze  standing stone ogham	*Barrow*: grave covered by mound of soil. *Fulacht fia*: A trench lined with wood and filled with water. The water was heated using hot rocks from a fire. Then meat wrapped in straw was cooked in the boiling water. *Standing stone*: just as the name suggests. Unsure of what they were for, maybe to mark boundaries, burials or had a ritual purpose. Also *stone rows, stone circles*. *Gallán*: Could have *ogham* written on them.

600 BC	Iron Age and Celtic	Warfare was common between the different Celtic tribes. They settled at places which were easy to defend. The materials used varied from place to place (stone, clay).	*Rath, ringfort*: enclosed farm where high circular banks of clay were built. (*Caiseal*: fort built of stone.) *Hillfort*: larger than ringfort, built on *hilltop*. *Promontory fort*: Built on *cliff edge* along coastal areas for defence. *Crannóg*: Built on an artificial island in a *lake*. *Togher*: A wooden route way built across a marshy area. *Souterrain*: an underground passage way.

Remains of a ringfort on the landscape, Portballintrae, Co. Antrim.

⚬ ringfort on OS maps

Lios ⎤	
Dun	
Rath	Ancient fort
Caher	
Cashel ⎦	

AD 500	**Early Christian**	First early Christian sites located in isolated scenic areas. The monks liked nature and the quiet surroundings *Lowland*: building and access easier *Fertile soils*: farming, source of food *River and forests*: timber and paper They provided services for religious and educational functions and also for trade. People began to settle around monasteries.	*church* ⎤ *monastery* All show *high cross* evidence of *cilin* monastic *Ch.* settlement. *Holy well* ⎦

cill ⎤ church
teampall ⎦

mainistir	monastery

Eighth and ninth centuries	**Viking**	Vikings came in the late eighth to ninth centuries. They raided monastic sites along *coastal* areas and moved inland up rivers. Later they settled at sites near *river estuaries*.	*Round towers*

fjord	ford

Twelfth and thirteenth centuries	Norman	Normans conquered and captured *Viking settlements*. *Defence and control* were important. Their settlements had to have both military and dwelling functions. *Castles* to protect captured land *River crossings, river bends, hilltops* Rivers: defence against attack, clean water, transport Norman settlers built houses near castles for security against attacks from the Irish.	*Motte and Bailey*: *Motte* or mound on which a wooden tower was built connected by means of a bridge to a courtyard or *bailey*. The whole area was surrounded by a water filled *moat*. *Castles*: stone defensive buildings replaced wooden towers which easily burnt down. *Town wall*
Twelfth century	Abbeys Christians mainistir monastery	To try and bring new life to the monastic life in Ireland European orders encouraged by Normans began to set up monasteries. They were *focal points* for settlement and urban areas grew around them. They provided education, farming, alms for the poor etc.	*Abbey* *Priory* *Friary*
Sixteenth and seventeenth centuries	Plantation	Plantation towns were planned. The first were in Laois and Offaly, e.g. Birr and Portlaoise. They have a regular layout; roads joining at right angles with buildings and gardens at uniform or same size. Squares may occur in the centres.	*Squares*
Eighteenth and nineteenth centuries	Demesnes	Large estates belonging to landlords with large mansions or castles with gardens and orchards. They located near *roads* and *urban settlement* to provide access and labour.	*Demesne*: large estate *Name of the estate*

There is a lot of evidence of past settlement on this map. To try and make sense of it all complete the grid below showing the time period, location and what each feature was used for.

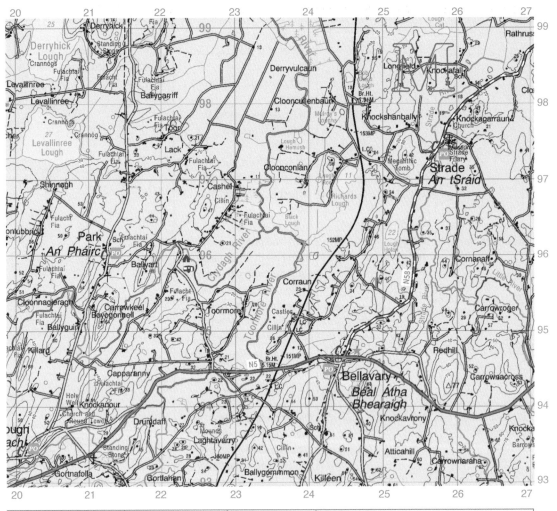

	Time	Feature	Grid Ref.	Explanation/usage
1.	Neolithic	Megalithic tomb	M 252 973	Burial chambers
2.	Bronze		M 214 934	Stones used to mark burial or boundary
		Fulachtaí fia		
3.			M 204 978	
		Rath		
4.	Early Christian			Small church
		Holy well		
5.	Viking			
6.		Castle		
7.	Christian	Friary	M 260 974	Part of a monastery

This area shows evidence of settlement right back to Neolithic times. Why do you think this is so?

There are a lot of fulachtaí fia in the north-west of the map. What were fulachtaí fia and why do you think there are so many around the loughs?

Why do you think the church and round tower were built at the site at **M 20 93**?

Summary: Fill in the blanks

Historic settlement is shown on OS maps by a_____ which are written in

r_____. Looking at where people chose to s_____ in the past can tell us

a lot about the development of t_____ and c_____.

The earliest settlers chose sites beside *water* such as r_____, l_____ and

c_____ sites. They gave water supplies for d_____ and c_____,

food and t_____.

With the arrival of the Celts, N_____ and V_____ *defence* and control

of captured land was important. They chose sites which were easy to defend in

times of w_____ or attack. This included h_____, bends in r_____

and cliff edges. In Norman times people settled in or around c_____ for

safety.

Religion played another important role in where people decided to live. People

settled near m_____. They gave help to the p_____, e_____, and

medical help. These sites then became t_____ centres.

Chapter 12
Settlement on Ordnance Survey maps

The term settlement means where people live. We have already looked at historic settlement; where people lived in the past.

In this chapter we will look at
- rural settlement
- settlement patterns
- urban settlement.

Houses are shown on OS maps as small black squares

Density of settlement means the number of houses in a square kilometre (km²). To calculate density of settlement count the number of houses in a grid square. (Each grid square is 1 km² in size.)

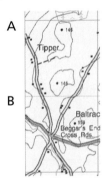

The density of settlement in grid square A is 12 per km².

What is the density of settlement of grid square B?
_____ per km²

Distribution of settlement is uneven on most maps; some areas will have a high density of settlement while other areas may have no settlement. Areas which people avoid living in are:

Upland areas because of
- poorer weather conditions
- soils are thinner
- harder to build on steep slopes

Poorly drained areas such as flood plains of rivers or the margins of lakes because of the danger of flooding.

Most people tend to live on *flat or gently sloping lands* that are well drained.
This is because:

- it is easier to build roads and houses
- there is better transport and access
- they generally have a more favourable climate
- soils are likely to be deeper and more fertile.

Settlement patterns

Rural settlement can be divided into three main patterns:

Linear: buildings are built in a line along the
sides of roads. They may be found at the
edges of towns or villages.

Nucleated: several houses are built close
together. This is most likely at the junction of
roads – where roads join – or bridging points.

Many nucleated settlements are villages which
have schools and churches for the community.

Dispersed: where individual buildings are found by
themselves with wide spaces in between. Found close to
roads, ends of tracks.

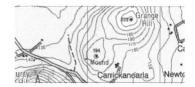

What settlement patterns are shown in A–C?

two types

A _____   B _____   C _____

Development of towns

Towns develop at certain locations for many reasons.

1. **Physical environment:**

   Towns favour low-lying, flat or gently sloping lands. They avoid upland areas because:
   - climate and soil conditions are generally better
   - easier to build roads and buildings.

2. **Route focus:**

   Where roads, rivers and other routeways meet. In the past trade may have developed at the meeting points of roads.

3. **Bridging points:**

   Roads may converge or meet at the bridge of a river and towns develop at this point.

4. **Historical factors:**

   Defence: defence was an important need during the troubled middle ages so people settled near castles, towers or inside walled towns for safety.

   Monasteries: were an important focus point and settlements developed near them as they gave medical help, help to the poor and provided education.

   Coasts: the first invaders and settlers in Ireland settled in coastal areas. They became important trading and fishing ports.

   Rivers: rivers catered for the needs of the early settler: food, water, means of transport and natural defence so many towns developed on the banks of rivers, some set back a little to avoid flooding.

Give three reasons why Drogheda developed at this location (9 marks).

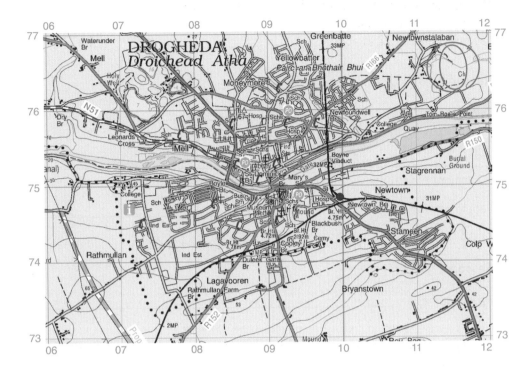

Sample answer

Drogheda has developed at this location for many reasons.

First reason

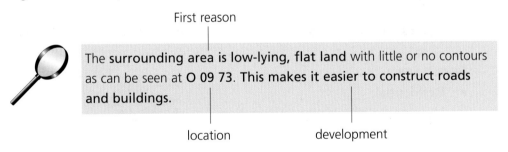

The **surrounding area is low-lying, flat land** with little or no contours as can be seen at **O 09 73. This makes it easier to construct roads and buildings.**

location   development

Drogheda is a **route focus**, with national routeways (N51) and regional routeways (R166, R150 and R152) leading into the town as can be seen at **O 08 75**. This helps the growth of trade in the town.

Drogheda in the past would have been a **defensive settlement**. This can be seen with the presence of a motte at **O 091 747** and two gates, one at **O 088 748**. This shows us Drogheda was a Norman town and people would have settled in or around the motte and bailey castle for safety in times of attack.

Over to you

Come up with two more reasons why Drogheda developed at this location.

Lay out your reasons as above.

Reason 1

Drogheda in the past _____. This can be seen with

reason

_____ . _____

location   development

People would have settled there because _____.

Reason 2

Drogheda has a _____

_____

_____

Urban functions

The *functions* of a town are the services and activities that benefit the people who live there or in the surrounding areas.

Functions

- **Residential:**
  Housing for people who may work in the area or in nearby cities.

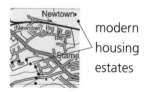 modern housing estates

- **Industrial:**
  Most towns have factories which provide employment. Industrial estates which have several factories and businesses are shown on OS maps.

- **Tourist:**

  An area may have a high *tourist potential* and is
  developed to take advantage of this.

  How has Crosshaven been developed to take
  advantage of its tourist potential?

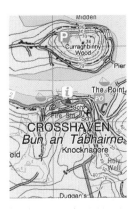

- **Services:**

  Most towns offer a wide range of services,
  such as hospital, colleges, schools, fire station,
  church, garda station.

  Some will not be shown on the OS map.

  Commercial: shops, banks

  Recreational: bars, cinemas, restaurants

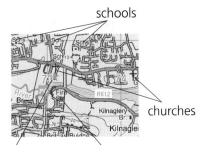

schools

churches

garda station   fire station

- **Historical:**

  The town may have had a past function. Evidence of this past function
  will be shown through antiquities or place names.

- **Defence:**

  Security was an important need so the presence of a castle or tower
  would have encouraged people to settle in the area.

- **Religious:**

  Monasteries were an important focus for settlement in the past as they
  would have given education, help to the poor etc. Shown by abbeys or
  priories in or around the town.

Chapter **13**
Locational geography

You may be asked in the exam to choose a suitable location for a factory, school, leisure centre or hotel on an OS map or photograph.

Location of a factory

Imagine you had to build a factory. What would you need to keep in mind?

1. **Good site:**
   Level land which is easy to build on and space to expand if business is good!

2. **Workers:**
   People to work for you; is there a town nearby to employ them from?

3. **Transport:**
   To get your workers to the factory! Roads, railways, ports to get your raw materials in and your product out.

4. **Market:**
   A town full of people to buy your product.

Look at the location of this factory in Dungarvan.

Coastal area: port nearby to help get raw materials in and export your product.

Good site: flat land makes it easier to build on.

Bridge: river does not limit access to other areas.

Other factories: may be able to help you in production costs.

Additional space: for storage, parking for workers, space to expand.

Town: nearby for workers and perhaps a market to sell your product to. Town will also have services such as banking which you will need.

Roads: for easy access and to transport your product.

But what are the disadvantages of locating the factory where it is?

1. **Pollution:**
   Waste may pollute the river. Air pollution caused by production and increased traffic noise pollution.

2. **Traffic congestion:**
   More traffic leads to congestion.

If you are asked to *select an industry* for an area look at the surrounding area and resources available. If there is a coastal area fish processing would be a good industry to choose. Forest: paper manufacturing; good farmland: food processing.

Location of a hotel or leisure centre

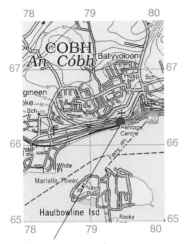

Space: to expand if necessary and for parking

Town: will provide customers and workers

Services: such as nightlife, shopping, church, garda station

Transport: railway, good roads to allow access for customers

Additional activities: here there is boating. The map shows a heritage centre

Historical sites: to attract potential customers

Location of a school

Space: for parking, extensions and playing fields

Access: good transport network for staff and students; safety considerations

Town: to provide staff and students

Services: in town for school administration, e.g. banking

Sites of interest: nearby to enhance teaching, e.g. castle, river for field studies

It has been proposed to build a large computer factory in the area covered by the OS map. Suggest a suitable site and give three reasons for your choice.

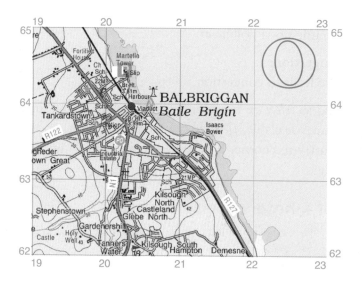

Sample answer

The site I would suggest for the location of a computer factory is at **O 197 632**, on the outskirts of the town at the industrial estate. The reasons why I would suggest this location are:

reason	location	development

1. It is **near the town** of Balbriggan at **O 20 63**. The town would **provide workers and also contain services** such as banking which the factory needs.

2. There is a good transport system. A railway at **O 204 640** and national and regional roads passing the site: NI and R122. This will allow easy access for workers and the transport of raw materials and finished product.

3. It is a site on flat, level land as shown with little or no contours: **O 19 62**. It is easier to build on this level land and there is enough space for future expansion, parking and storage.

Give one disadvantage of locating at this area.

Sample answer

One disadvantage of locating at this site is that it may give rise to increased **traffic congestion** which will increase levels of **air pollution**.

It has been proposed to build a hotel in the area covered by the OS map.
Suggest a suitable site and give three reasons for your choice.

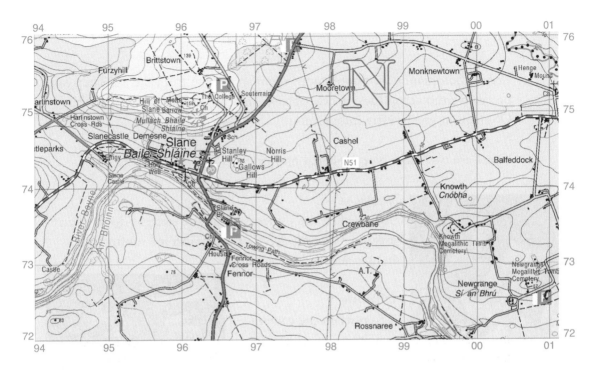

Answer outline

The site I would suggest is located at _____

                       reason   location

Reason 1:   The **village of Slane** is at _____ which would provide

           w_____ and services for the customer such as _____

           development   activities

Reason 2: *(your own reason)*

_____

_____

Reason 3: *(your own reason)*

_____

_____

One disadvantage of locating in this area: _____

_____

Chapter **14**
Aerial photographs

Aerial photographs are photographs of an area taken from the air. They can be taken from aeroplanes or helicopters. They are useful when used with OS maps in giving extra information.

There are two main types of aerial photos:

Vertical
Taken when the camera is pointing straight down at an area (like a bird's eye view). You can see rooftops of houses and buildings.

Oblique
Taken when the camera is pointing at an angle. You can see heights of buildings or their fronts.

Are photographs I to V vertical or oblique?

Photo I (page 109)   _____

Photo II (page 112)   _____

Photo III (page 115)   _____

Photo IV (page 118)   _____

Photo V (page 121)   _____

It is important to know the difference between the two when you are giving the location of features on an aerial photograph. No matter if it is a vertical or an oblique photograph you divide the photo into a grid of nine squares.

Vertical when a north direction arrow is shown

Compass directions are used.

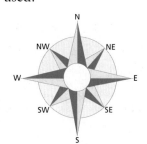

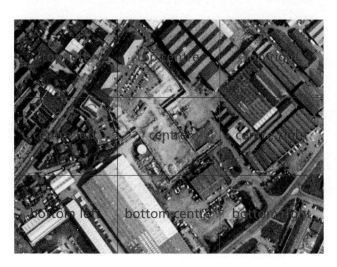

Vertical when no direction arrow is given

The rows of the grid are called top, centre and bottom.

Oblique photographs

The photo is taken at an angle. The area closest to the camera lens, to the front, is known as the foreground and the area furthest away, at the back, is the background.

Recognising features on photographs

historical site   shops   bridge   railway station

green area/gardens   parking   church   remains of church   loading   marina
                                              historical site   crane

Look at the map of Waterford. What is the name of the bridge in the centre background of the photograph?

_____

Give the location for the following features:

1.	Railway station	**right background**
2.	Remains of church	
3.	Green area/gardens	
4.	Shops	
5.	Parking	

Locating features on vertical photographs

Label the vertical photograph with the features below. Use the map to help you. Give the locations of each feature.

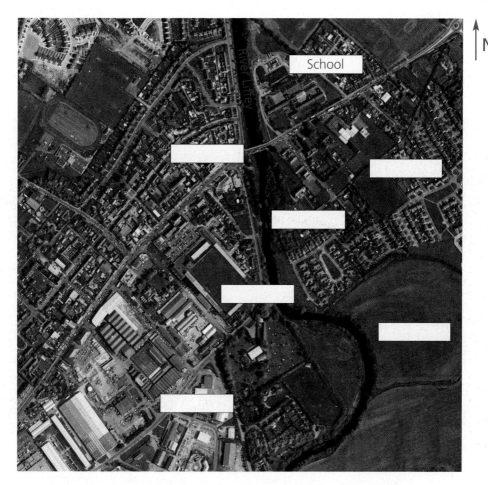

1.	School	North-east
2.	Bridge	
3.	Industrial estate	
4.	Sports ground	
5.	Housing estate	
6.	River meander	
7.	Deciduous trees	

Colour and photographs

Colour on photographs can give us a lot more information than you think! It can tell us things like what type of farming activity is being carried out in fields.

brown: ploughed fields ready for crops

yellow/light green: arable farming used to grow crops

blue: rivers, canals, lakes, sea

grey: roads

dark green: pastoral farming for animals to graze. Also shows green spaces/gardens in towns.

Time of year and photographs

You can even tell sometimes the *time of year* a photo was taken (especially if the photograph has some countryside in it).

 Wintertime

ploughed fields ready for planting in spring

Sometimes you may be able to see smoke rising from chimneys.

no farm animals in fields

trees and bushes are bare with no leaves

Summertime

trees and bushes are green with leaves (*foliage*)

farm animals grazing in fields

Sometimes you may be able to see hay bales in fields.

fields light green or yellow with ripe cereals

Locating features: Drogheda

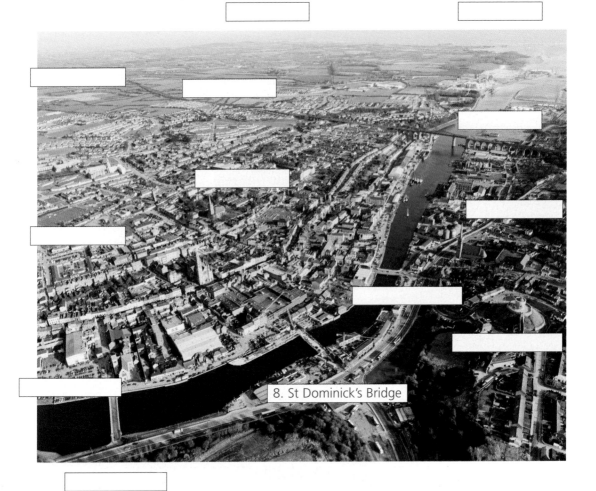

8. St Dominick's Bridge

1. What time of year was this photograph taken? _____

2. Give two reasons for your answer.
   a) _____
   b) _____

Label the photograph of Drogheda using the features below. Use the map to help find the bridge names. Give the location for each feature.

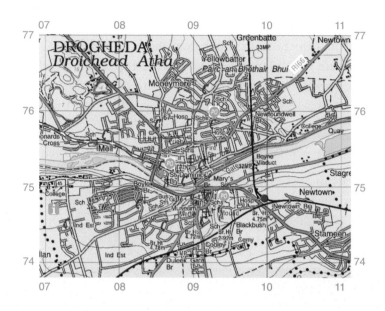

1.	Housing estate	
2.	Ploughed fields	
3.	Agricultural Land	
4.	Estuary	**right background**
5.	Railway bridge/Boyne viaduct	
6.	St Mary's Bridge	
7.	Boyle Bridge	
8.	St Dominick's Bridge	
9.	Motte	
10.	Shopping centre	
11.	Playing fields	
12.	Church	
13.	Industrial estate	

Distance and photographs

As we have seen on OS maps the scale is the same throughout the map extract so we can measure distances between areas with confidence.

The same cannot be said for *oblique* photographs as the scale changes. Features near the camera seem larger than those further away.

So to calculate the distance between two features we need the help of the Ordnance Survey map of the area. It's quite easy to do.

You have been asked to calculate the distance between the two churches in Clifden.

- First locate the two features on your photo and map: (+ church)

- Measure the distance between the two on the map
  (using straight line distance) (if less than 1 km place on the linear scale
  km which is divided into 1/10ths)

Answer: 0.4 km

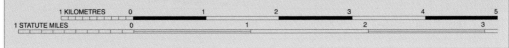

Camera direction

Finding camera direction on vertical photographs

If a direction arrow is given on a photograph which shows north it can be quite easy to work out direction.

Finding camera direction on oblique photographs

If no direction arrow is given your OS map will help. Again you need to locate features on your photo that are clearly recognisable on the map, e.g. bridges, quays, headlands, inlets, lakes.

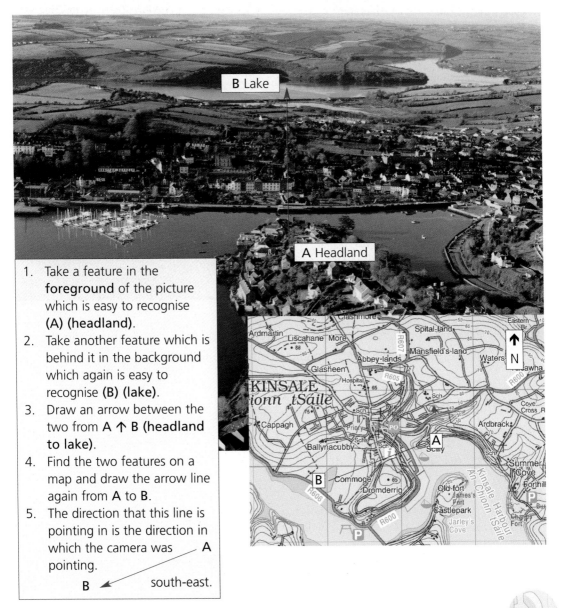

1. Take a feature in the **foreground** of the picture which is easy to recognise **(A) (headland)**.
2. Take another feature which is behind it in the background which again is easy to recognise **(B) (lake)**.
3. Draw an arrow between the two from **A ↑ B (headland to lake)**.
4. Find the two features on a map and draw the arrow line again from **A** to **B**.
5. The direction that this line is pointing in is the direction in which the camera was pointing.

south-east.

Sketch map of photograph

You have been asked to draw a sketch map of Askeaton as shown on the aerial photograph. Mark on and identify the following:

- the river
- a reservoir of water
- residential area
- a castle in ruins
- two connecting roads.

So how do you go about drawing your sketch map?

Step 1

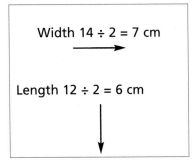

Width 14 ÷ 2 = 7 cm

Length 12 ÷ 2 = 6 cm

Draw the frame of your sketch map. It is to be *smaller* but of the *same shape* as the photo. A handy guide is to draw it quarter the size (measure length and width and divide by 2).

Step 2

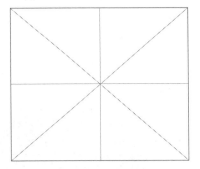

Draw in guidelines lightly on both the photo and your frame to help you place features.

Step 3

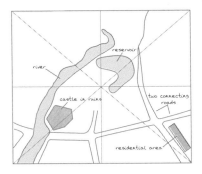

Draw in the coastline (if any), draw in each feature you have been asked to mark and *name* them.

Step 4

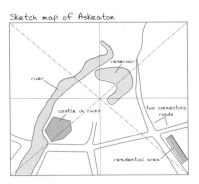

Give your sketch a title and direction arrow if there is one on the photo.

Tips

- Always use a pencil and ruler.
- Always label or name your features.
- Only draw what you have been asked to identify in the question.
- To draw your features draw an outline or boundary to the same shape as in the photo (see below).

Marking ✓
Total: 12 marks

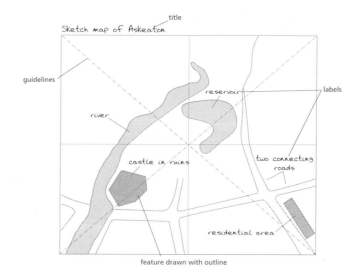

title

Sketch map of Askeaton

guidelines

river

reservoir

labels

castle in ruins

two connecting roads

residential area

feature drawn with outline

Former settlement

In Chapter 11 we looked at *antiquities*, how they help us to understand the development of a town and why our ancestors chose to settle where they did.

Some of these antiquities can be seen clearly on aerial photographs, especially if they were made of stone. But some, such as fulachtaí fia and souterrains, are difficult to spot.

Raised circular banks of clay show a ringfort. The people who built this fort may have chosen the coastal location as it was a source of water, food and transport.

Remains of castle in the centre of the photo. The site may have been chosen as the river would have been a source of food, water and transport and also for defensive purposes.

Urban functions

The *functions* of a town are the services and activities that benefit the people who live there or in surrounding areas. Many of these functions can be clearly seen on aerial photographs.

Residential: housing estate

Religious: convent, church

Industrial: factory

Commercial: shops, bars

Recreational: boating, restaurants, bars

Tourist: boating, parking, bars, restaurants

Not all the functions in Cobh have been shown. Match the function in the box below to the evidence that may be seen in the photo.

Recreational Port Services Transport Educational Defence		
	roads, railways **(route focus)**	_____
	playing fields, parks, racecourses	_____
	schools, colleges	_____
	castle, town walls, towers	_____
	fire station, garda station	_____
	docks, cargo ships, ships, boats	_____

Complete the sample answer

Give three functions for Askeaton as shown in the aerial photograph on page 86. Give evidence from the photograph.

location / evidence   statement

One urban function provided by Askeaton **is residential** as can be seen by the **row of houses in the right foreground.** This provides accommodation for those **who work in or near the town and who will use the services provided.**

explanation

A former function of Askeaton was defence as can be seen by _____

_____

_____

_____

A third function is _____

_____

_____

_____

Economic activities

By looking at the features and land usage on a map you can see how people make their living in the area or what the economic activities are.

Primary activities are those which involve taking natural resources (crops, fish, trees) from the land or sea. Examples include:
- *farming*: look for agricultural land, ploughed fields, animals etc.
- *fishing*: look for quays, boats
- *forestry*: look for a big area of tree cover.

Secondary activities are those in which people process, make or manufacture products. They may take natural resources (trees to make into planks of wood) or change materials further (make planks into furniture). Evidence on maps would include industrial estates and warehouses.

Tertiary activities are those which provide useful services such as shops, banks and restaurants.

Evidence on maps will include shop fronts, shopping centres and market squares.

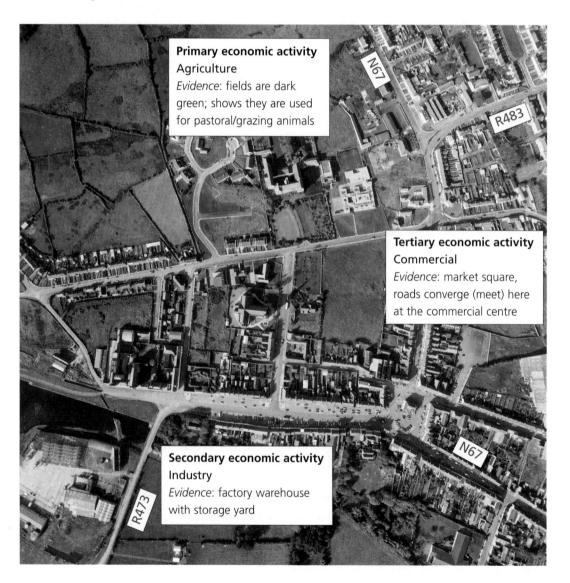

Primary economic activity
Agriculture
Evidence: fields are dark green; shows they are used for pastoral/grazing animals

Tertiary economic activity
Commercial
Evidence: market square, roads converge (meet) here at the commercial centre

Secondary economic activity
Industry
Evidence: factory warehouse with storage yard

Look at the photo of Drogheda on page 82. What types of economic activity are being carried out in the area? Give photo evidence in your answer.

economic activity   evidence

Primary economic activities are being carried out in the Drogheda area such as **agriculture and fishing**. Agriculture can be seen in the **background** of the photo, with **freshly ploughed brown fields in the centre background ready for the planting of crops**. There are also darker green fields nearby which would be used for pastoral farming and the grazing of animals. Fishing may also be carried out as shown by the presence of boats in the right centre.

explanation / development

Secondary activities are being carried out at _____.

_____

_____

Finally, evidence of tertiary activities can be seen at _____.

_____

_____

Urban settlement on photographs

By looking at map evidence it may be possible to say why a town developed where it did. We have already looked at this in Chapter 12. Towns develop at areas which have:-

Flat or gently sloping land: it is easier and cheaper to build buildings or roads on flat land. Also people tend to avoid upland areas due to poorer soil and poorer weather conditions.

Rivers: in the past people may have located near riversides for water supply and transport reasons. Also bends in rivers – meanders – would have been easier to *defend*.

Route focus: where roads meet or converge such as the *bridging points of rivers*: people would have met here for trade and markets.

Coastal areas: the sea would have provided water and food. Towns may have grown around a fishing industry.

Historical: photos may show the remains of castles, walls or gates which show the town may have developed for *defensive reasons*. Also they may have remains of abbeys or priories, which show that a monastery may have been there in the past.

Look at the photo below of Clifden.

1. Why do you think there is little settlement in the right background?

_____

_____

2. Give three reasons why you think Clifden developed at this location.

evidence   reason

One reason why Clifden developed at this location is because it is **gently sloping land at the base of an upland area as seen in the right background**. It is **easier and cheaper to build roads and buildings on flat or gently sloping land**.

explanation

Another reason may be that Clifden is a route focus as can be seen _____ .

_____

_____

Finally _____ .

_____

_____

Traffic problems

With the increase in car ownership in Ireland there has been an increase in traffic problems and congestion in towns and cities. As a result different ways of allowing the traffic to move about quickly and more easily in built-up areas have to be put in place: **traffic management**.

Places where traffic builds up and causes congestion include:

Main shopping areas (central business district) People try and get as close as they can to the shops and services such as banks and hairdressers, to save time and to carry their purchases a shorter distance.

Where streets meet or converge such as crossroads or bridging points. Many cars all trying to pass the one point causes problems such as traffic jams or accidents.

Where streets narrow traffic has to pass slowly and carefully so as not to cause damage to parked or passing cars.

So what is done to allow traffic to move quickly and easily? *Road markings* such as stop lines and arrows make it easy for motorists to understand the traffic regulations.

One way streets allow the free movement of traffic.

Yellow boxes allow traffic to merge quickly and safely.

Parking: double yellow lines allow enough space for the free movement of traffic. Car parks may be provided to help with parking problems, or if streets are wide enough roadside parking may be allowed.

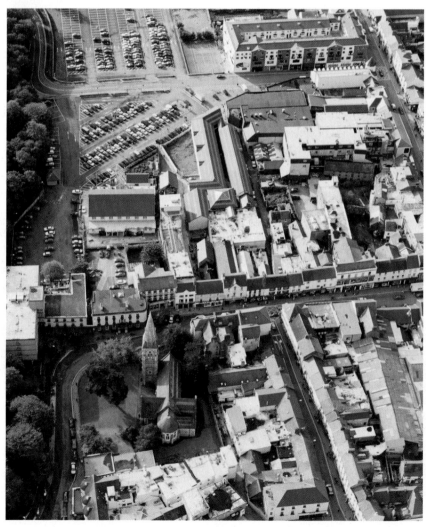

Other ways of managing traffic

- *Traffic islands* help in breaking up traffic lanes, making it clear where traffic lanes lead.

- *Roundabouts* allow the free movement of traffic where busy roads meet.

- *Bypasses* (shown on OS maps): major routeways such as motorways or national roads are built around a town and divert traffic which does not need to pass through a busy town away from it.

- *Traffic lights* regulate the safe movement of traffic at junctions.

A. Look at the oblique photograph of Westport on page 98 and give two locations where traffic problems might occur.

B. Using evidence from the photograph describe three measures which have been taken in order to deal with motor traffic in the town.

A. Traffic problems

location   statement

1. One location where traffic problems may happen is at the **bridging point of the river** _____ in the **centre background**. This will cause problems as **there are several roads converging at this one point, which may lead to congestion and accidents.**

explanation / development

2. Another location where traffic problems may occur is at _____

_____ in the _____ of the photo.

This will cause problems as _____

_____

B. Traffic measures

Measures which have been taken in order to deal with motor traffic in the town are:

statement   location   explanation / development

1. The use of a **one-way system** at the **left centre. This allows for the free movement of traffic in two lanes leaving the town centre.**

2. _____

    _____

3. _____

    _____

Urban planning

Photographs of towns may show evidence of planning in the way they have been built or laid out. They may be new towns or suburbs which have grown to accommodate commuters. Urban planners try to make an area more pleasant and convenient for residents to live in.

How you may recognise urban planning

Street patterns will join at right angles to form a 'grid iron' system.

Traffic management as described on page 96. Here there are car parks, bridges and road markings.

Buildings will be in orderly patterns. Estate gardens will be the same size or have a uniform pattern.

Green areas, parks with walkways, public gardens, playing fields will allow for recreation.

Trees and shrubbery planted to improve appearance and give shade.

Also present may be:

- *Shopping centres* to take traffic out of town centres and ease congestion.
- *Use of zones* for different functions such as residential (housing estates), industry (industrial estates).

Look at the aerial photograph of Waterford.

Describe *three* ways in which the area has benefited from town planning.

statement   location

1. One way in which the area has benefited from town planning is the use of **green areas** as can be found in the **centre background**. This **provides a recreational area for those living in the nearby housing estate.**

development / explanation

2. A second way town planning can be seen is _____

_____.

3. A third way _____

_____.

Chapter **16**
Homework or classwork activities

Directions

Naas (Map I, page 108)

1. What river flows to the south of the map? _____

2. What small village is to the south-west of Naas? _____

3. The M7 ( ), which goes from the west of Naas to the edge of
    the map, runs from

    north-east to south-east ☐   north to south ☐

    south-west to north-east ☐   south-east to north-east ☐

4. In what direction from the post office (PO) outside Two Mile House is
    Punchestown?

Westport (Map II, page 111)

1. What river enters Westport to the south-east? _____

2. In what direction from the post office in Westport is Ballin Lough?

    _____

3. In what direction from the post office in Westport is Cross Lough?

    _____

Killarney (Map III, page 114)

1. In what direction is Tomies Mountain from Killarney town?

    north-east ☐   north-west ☐

    south-west ☐   south ☐

2. In what direction is Tomies Wood from Innisfallen in Lough Leane?

    north-east ☐   south-east ☐

    south-west ☐   north ☐

3. What river flows to the south of Killarney? _____

Dungarvan (Map IV, page 117)

1. What main river flows in the north-west of the map? _____.

2. What road enters Dungarvan town from a north-westerly direction?
   R_____. ━━━━━━━━━━

3. In what direction from Crohaun Mountain is Dungarvan?
   _____.

4. In what direction from Crohaun Mountain is Shandon Island?
   _____.

Clifden (Map V, page 120)

1. What village is to the north-east of Clifden? _____.

2. What river flows to the north of Letterfrack? _____.

3. In what direction from Lough Auna is Letterfrack?
   north-west ☐   south-east ☐
   north-east ☐   west ☐

4. In what direction from Lough Auna is Barnaderg Bay?
   north ☐   south-west ☐
   south ☐   north-east ☐

Scale and measuring distance

Naas (Map I, page 108)

1. What is the length of the map in km?

2. What is the width of the map in km?

3. What is the distance in km from the post office in Naas to the post office outside Two Mile House?

4. Measure the distance in km along the M7 from the north of the map until it leaves in the west of the map.

Westport (Map II, page 111)

1. What is the distance in km from the parking (P) at Westport Quay to the post office in Westport?

2. Measure the distance in km along the N5 road (━━) from Westport town centre until it leaves the map to the east.

Killarney (Map III, page 114)

1. What is the distance in km from the parking at Muckross in the south of the map to the post office in Killarney?

2. Measure the distance in km along the N72 (━■━■━) in the north-west of the map until it reaches the garda station in Killarney (★).

Dungarvan (Map IV, page 117)

1. What is the distance in km from the post office in Dungarvan to the parking to the north?

2. Measure the distance in km along the N72 to the north of Dungarvan until it meets the N25.

Clifden (Map V, page 120)

1. What is the distance in km from the post office in Clifden to the post office in Letterfrack?

Area

Naas (Map I, page 108)

Calculate the area in km² of this map extract.

Westport (Map II, page 111)

Calculate the area in km² covered by Westport Bay in the west of the map.

Killarney (Map III, page 114)

Calculate the area in km² of the area covered by Lough Leane.

Dungarvan (Map IV, page 117)

Calculate the area in km² of the land above 200 m in the north (yellow and brown).

Clifden (Map V, page 120)

Calculate the area in km² of the area covered by Ballynakill Harbour.

Grid references

Naas (Map I, page 108)

1. Give a four-figure grid reference for the following features:
   Punchestown Racecourse _____
   Broadfield _____

2. Give a six-figure grid reference for the following features:
   Jigginstown House _____
   moated site at Two Mile House _____
   post office outside Two Mile House _____

3. What feature is located at the following grid reference?
   N 906 164   barrow ☐   post office ☐
   standing stone ☐   graveyard ☐

4. What feature is located at the following grid reference?
   N 874 133   church ☐   castle ☐
   holy well ☐   post office ☐

Westport (Map II, page 111)

1. Give a four-figure grid reference for the following features:
   Clogher Lough _____
   Westport Quay _____

2. Give a six-figure grid reference for the following features:
   post office in Westport _____
   railway station in the south-east _____
   crannóg in Ballin Lough _____

3. What feature is located at the following grid reference?
   L 996 879   church ☐   graveyard ☐
   crannóg ☐   railway station ☐

4. What feature is located at the following grid reference?
   L 971 856   holy well ☐   golf course ☐
   post office ☐   parking ☐

Symbols

Naas (Map I, page 108)

1. At which one of the following grid references will you find a Garda Síochána (police) station?

   N 89 19 ☐   N 87 17 ☐

   N 89 18 ☐   N 90 19 ☐

2. The feature located at N 912 179 is a

   post office ☐   train station ☐

   public telephone ☐   golf course ☐

3. The feature located at N 919 159 is a

   viewpoint ☐   airfield ☐

   post office ☐   airport ☐

Westport (Map II, page 111)

1. At which one of the following grid references will you find a tourist information centre?

   L 99 84 ☐   M 00 84 ☐

   L 00 83 ☐   M 01 83 ☐

2. There is a youth hostel at grid reference M 006 842. The symbol used to show this is

   a red circle ☐   a red triangle ☐

   a black square ☐   a blue triangle ☐

3. In the boxes provided match each letter in column X with the number of its pair in column Y. One pair has been completed for you.

X	
A	L 97 85
B	L 94 85
C	M 00 84
D	L 98 85
E	L 93 87

Y	
1	Caravan site
2	Boating activities
3	Telephone
4	Youth hostel
5	Golf course

A	
B	
C	4
D	
E	

Killarney (Map III, page 114)

1. How many parking symbols are shown on the map?

   15 ☐   10 ☐   20 ☐   9 ☐

2. What feature is shown at the following location?

   V 970 864   viewpoint ☐   parking ☐

   picnic site ☐   camping ☐

3. In the boxes provided match each letter in column X with the number of its pair in column Y. One pair has been completed for you.

X	
A	V 98 88
B	V 92 91
C	V 90 90
D	V 95 89
E	V 93 89

Y	
1	Youth hostel
2	Boating activities
3	Inisfallen
4	Golf course
5	Nature reserve

A	
B	
C	2
D	
E	

Dungarvan (Map IV, page 117)

1. Measure the distance in km from the viewpoint at S 278 019 to the golf course at X 285 954. _____ km

2. What type of woodland is located at the following grid reference?
   S 25 01   mixed ☐   coniferous ☐   natural ☐

3. In the boxes provided match each letter in column X with the number of its pair in column Y. One pair has been completed for you.

X	
A	S 274 009
B	X 265 937
C	X 262 930
D	S 278 019
E	X 236 981

Y	
1	Tourist information
2	Viewpoint
3	Public telephone
4	TV mast
5	Ringfort

A	
B	
C	
D	2
E	

Naas (Map I, page 108)

Ordnance Survey map

1. Draw a sketch map of the area shown on the Ordnance Survey map. Mark on and identify the following:
   - one built-up area
   - River Liffey
   - motorway
   - Grand Canal
   - golf course

2. Explain *three* reasons why Naas developed at this location.

3. Measure the distance in km along the R445 from its junction with the R409 at N 886 193 until it leaves the map at N 850 185.

(Photograph I, page 109)

Aerial photograph

1. Draw a sketch map of the area shown. Mark on and identify
   - the canal
   - two connecting roads
   - residential area
   - Central Business District (CBD)
   - parking

2. On your sketch map identify with the letter 'T' two places where traffic congestion may take place. Explain why there is likely to be traffic congestion at these areas.

   Using both Ordnance Survey map and aerial photograph give *three* ways in which attempts are being made to ease traffic congestion in Naas.

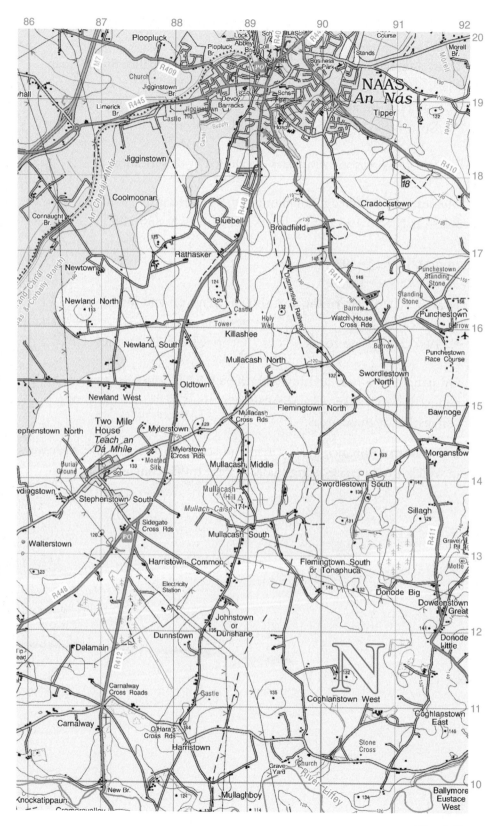

Map I: Naas

Photograph I: Naas

Westport (Map II, page 111)

Ordnance Survey map

1. Draw a sketch map of the area shown on the Ordnance Survey map. Mark on and identify

   - the coast
   - a town
   - national primary route
   - railway line
   - a river

   (Make sure to include a frame, title or heading and direction arrow on your sketch map.)

2. Using map evidence show how drainage has affected the construction of roads in the Westport area.

3. Examine the aerial photograph and the Ordnance Survey map. Name and describe *three* services provided by the town of Westport. You may use both the map and the aerial photograph or the map only.

(Photograph II, page 112)

Aerial photograph

1. Using the photograph draw a sketch map of the part of Westport town shown. Mark and identify the following:

   - the river
   - main road network
   - factory with storage yard
   - town square
   - modern housing estate

2. Look at the aerial photograph. Describe *three* ways in which the town has benefited from urban planning.

3. Using photograph and map evidence, outline an argument for and against building a hotel at the place labelled X on the photograph.

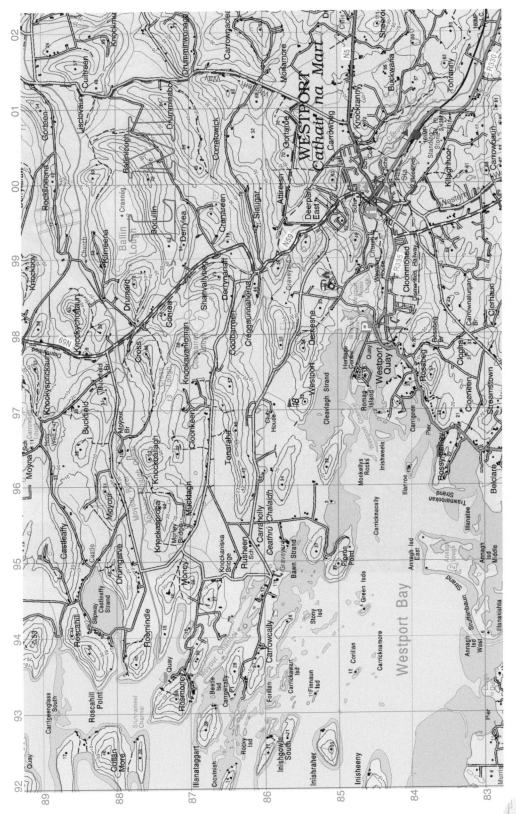

Map II: Westport

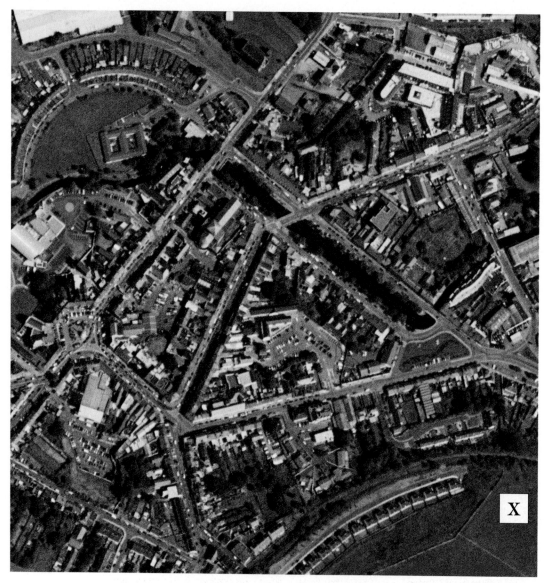

Photograph II: Westport

Killarney (Map III, page 114)
Ordnance Survey map

1. Draw a sketch map of the area shown on the Ordnance Survey map.
   Mark on and identify
   - one town
   - nature reserve
   - Lough Leane
   - upland above 200 m
   - national primary route

2. What evidence is on the map to suggest that Killarney is a tourist resort?

3. a) Imagine that you have climbed from Gortadirra (V 903 875) to the highest point on Tomies Mountain. What height would you have climbed?

   b) Measure the distance in km along the N71 from the junction with the N72 in Killarney town centre, V 966 905, to the junction at the post office at Cloghereen, V 978 875.

(Photograph III, page 115)
Aerial photograph

1. Draw a sketch map of the area shown on the aerial photograph.
   Mark on and identify
   - two connecting roads
   - church
   - modern housing estate
   - pastoral land use
   - woodland

2. What types of economic activity are being carried out in the area? Use both map and photograph evidence in your answer.

3. Where on the photograph would you propose to build a secondary school? Give *three* advantages of locating in the area which you have chosen using aerial photograph evidence only.

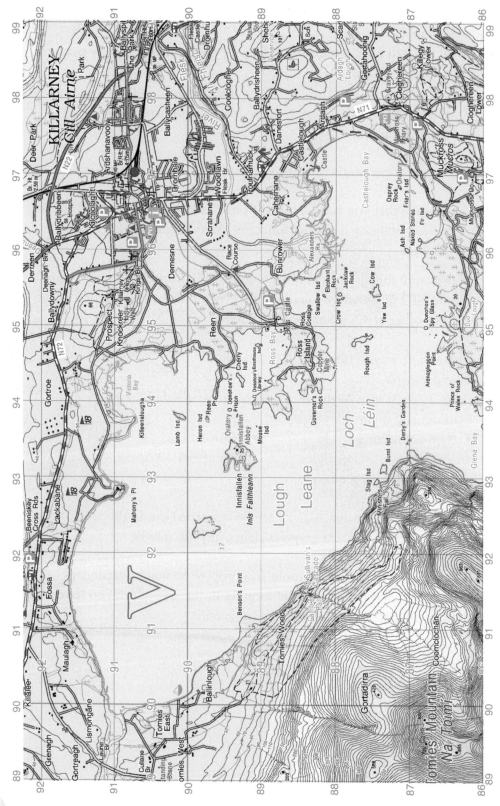

Map III: Killarney

Photograph III: Killarney

Dungarvan (Map IV, page 117)

Ordnance Survey map

1. Draw a sketch map of the area shown on the Ordnance Survey map. Mark on and identify
   - the coast
   - two national routes
   - golf course
   - land above 200 m
   - the built-up areas of Dungarvan

2. Imagine you are on holidays in Dungarvan. Write a postcard to a friend and on it list *four* of the attractions or facilities which are shown on the map.

3. Give *three* reasons why Dungarvan developed at this location. Use both map and photograph evidence.

(Photograph IV, page 118)

Aerial photograph

1. Draw a sketch map of the area shown on the aerial photograph. Mark on and identify
   - a river
   - pastural farming
   - two connecting roads
   - industrial land use
   - town square

2. Give *three* ways in which attempts are being made to tackle traffic problems in Dungarvan using photograph evidence only.

3. Give *three* functions for Dungarvan as shown in the aerial photograph.

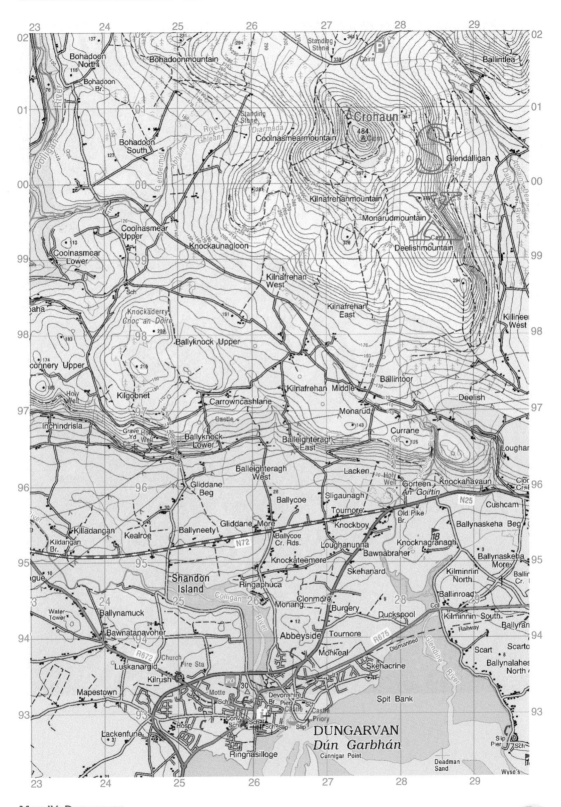

Map IV: Dungarvan

Photograph IV: Dungarvan

Clifden (Map V, page 120)

Ordnance Survey map

1. Draw a sketch map of the area shown by the Ordnance Survey map. Mark on and identify
   - coast
   - national secondary route
   - beach
   - two towns
   - one river

2. What is the shortest distance from Letterfrack to Clifden? (straight line distance) _____

   Why does the N59 not take this route? _____

3. What evidence of historic settlement is shown around Ballynakill Harbour and why do you think this location was chosen?

(Photograph V, page 121)

Aerial photograph

1. Draw a sketch map of the area shown on the aerial photograph. Mark on and identify
   - two connecting roads
   - shopping area
   - derelict building
   - church and convent
   - school

2. Using both map and photograph evidence list and explain *three* services provided by Clifden.

3. Suggest a location for the building of a small chemical production plant on the photograph. Give reasons for your choice of location.
   Outline one objection that may be proposed by the residents of Clifden.

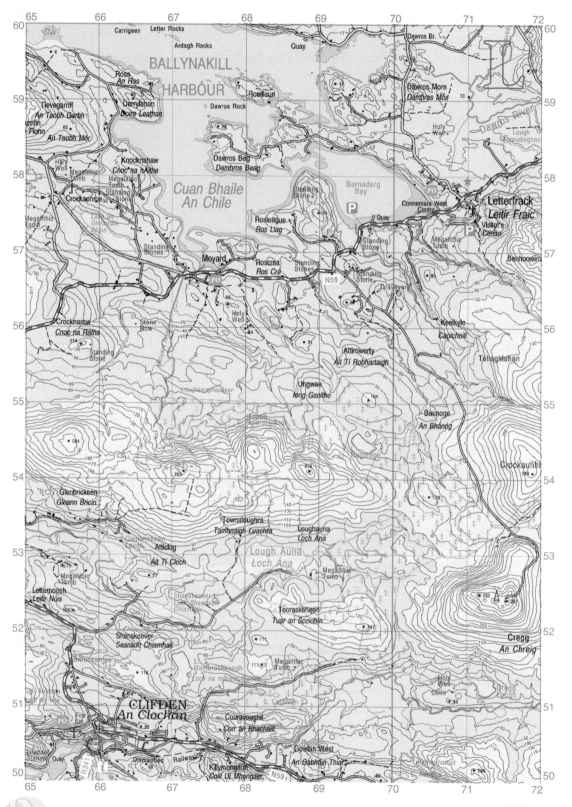

Map V: Clifden

Photograph V: Clifden